Good Housekeeping

Great Cakes

Good Housekeeping

Great Cakes

COLLINS & BROWN

First published in the United Kingdom in 2006 by
Collins & Brown
10 Southcombe Street
London W14 0RA

An imprint of Anova Books Company Ltd.

The *Good Housekeeping* website address is
www.allaboutyou.com/goodhousekeeping

3 4 5 6 7 8 9

ISBN 9781843403708

A catalogue record for this book is available from the
British Library.

Reproduction by Anorax Imaging Ltd, Leeds
Printed and bound by Toppan Leefung Printing Ltd, China

This book can be ordered direct from the publisher at
www.anovabooks.com

Note that certain recipes contain raw or lightly
cooked eggs. The young, elderly, pregnant women
and anyone with immune-deficiency disease should
avoid these, because of the slight risk of salmonella.

CONTENTS

Introduction

Baking was a weekly event in my nanny's house. Every Friday she would make not just one cake but several and keep them wrapped tightly in foil in the biscuit tin. It wasn't that my grandad had an insatiable appetite – she just liked to be prepared should anyone drop by unexpectedly. Because of the treats available I relished going there and it's no great surprise that I've grown up thinking I was born with a sweet tooth.

Then I came to work at Good Housekeeping where the team was in the middle of testing recipes for a baking feature. Every day at four on the dot a freshly sliced cake would appear in the office for us to try and give the nod of approval to. It certainly perked everyone up when that mid-afternoon energy slump hit. This inspirational book is full of ideas to try and enjoy - from tea-time treats and chocolate recipes to special celebration cakes. All the recipes have been triple tested in the Good Housekeeping Institute, so no matter what occasion you're making them for they'll work every time. My favourite is the Lemon Seed Loaf – let me know which is yours. Happy cooking!

Emma

Emma Marsden
Cookery Editor
Good Housekeeping

Left: Italian Ice Cream Cake, page 157

Baking

The key to successful baking lies in using good quality ingredients at the right temperature, measuring them accurately – using scales and measuring spoons – and following recipes carefully. Weigh out all of the ingredients before you start, using either metric or imperial measures, never a combination of the two. Make sure that you have the correct cake tin – the tin size quoted in the recipes refers to the base measurement – and take care to line the tin properly where necessary. Allow at least 15 minutes to heat the oven to the correct oven temperature.

Ingredients

Unsalted butter, rich and creamy in flavour, gives the best results in most recipes. Margarine can be substituted in many recipes although it doesn't lend such a good flavour, but low-fat 'spreads' with their high water content are not suitable. For most cake recipes, you need to use the fat at room temperature. If necessary, you can soften it, cautiously, in the microwave.

Eggs should also be used at room temperature; if taken straight from the fridge they are more likely to curdle a cake mixture. Make sure you use the correct size, too – unless otherwise stated, medium eggs should be used in all of these recipes.

Golden caster sugar is generally used for cakes, but light or dark muscovado sugars can be substituted for a richer colour and flavour.

Self-raising white flour is used in most cake recipes as it provides a raising agent, whereas plain white flour is generally used for biscuits and cookies. Plain or self-raising wholemeal flour can be substituted although the results will be darker, denser and nuttier in flavour. Half white and half wholemeal makes a good compromise if you want to incorporate extra fibre. If you sieve it before use, tip the bran left in the sieve into the bowl.

Check that other storecupboard ingredients to be included – such as nuts, dried fruits, extracts and spices – are well within their 'use-by' date.

Equipment

Little is needed in the way of special cake-making equipment for these recipes, other than scales, bowls, spoons, etc. However, a hand-held electric whisk is most useful as it takes all the effort out of creaming and whisking, and if you bake frequently, you will find that a free-standing electric mixer is a good investment. A food processor is perfect for rubbing fat into flour – for scones, biscuits, etc.

Good quality cake tins are essential, and non-stick tins are particularly useful. Sturdy baking sheets are important too. Choose ones that are large (but fit comfortably into your oven) to avoid baking in several batches.

Baking

Bake the cake mixture as soon as you have made it, as the raising agents will start to react straightaway. Once the cake is in the oven, resist the temptation to open the door – a sudden gush of cold air will make a part-baked cake sink. Instead, wait until the cooking time is almost up before testing. If your cake appears to be browning too quickly, cover the top loosely with greaseproof paper towards the end of cooking.

Apart from very light sponges, all cakes are best left to stand in their tin for 5–10 minutes after baking to firm up slightly. Biscuits, with their high sugar content, will seem very soft after baking. These too, should be left on the baking sheet for a few minutes before transferring to a wire rack.

Storage

With the exception of rich fruit cakes and gingerbread, most cakes and biscuits are best enjoyed freshly baked. If storing is necessary, use a cake tin or large plastic container. Make sure that the cake is completely cold before you put it into the container. If you haven't a large enough container, wrap in a double layer of greaseproof paper and overwrap with foil. Avoid putting rich fruit cakes in direct contact with foil; the fruit may react with it. Biscuits should never be stored in the same tin as a cake, and preferably not with other types of biscuits, as they quickly soften and absorb other flavours.

Most cakes, particularly sponges, freeze well, but they are generally best frozen before filling and decorating. If freezing a finished gateau, open-freeze first, then pack in a rigid container.

What if it isn't a success?

Unfortunately, it's not always easy to determine why a cake hasn't turned out as expected. Here are some possible reasons:

A close, dense texture may be the result of using too much liquid, too little raising agent, or an ineffective raising agent that is past its 'use-by' date. It may also be the outcome if the mixture curdled during creaming, or if the flour was folded in too vigorously.

A peaked, cracked top often occurs if the oven was too hot, or the cake was too near the top of the oven. Or it may be due to insufficient liquid, or using a tin which is too small.

If a cake sinks in the middle it is most likely to be because the oven door was opened too soon. Alternatively, it may be because ingredients haven't been measured accurately, or the wrong size cake tin may have been used.

Sunken fruit in a fruit cake occurs if the mixture is too soft to support the weight of the fruit. This is liable to happen if the fruit was too sticky or wet.

If the cake is heavy there may be too much liquid or not enough raising agent, or you haven't creamed the fat and sugar together sufficiently.

Preparation Techniques

Successful baking is at least partly dependant on the use of good basic techniques, such as lining and filling tins, whisking, folding in, etc.

Lining a round tin

Preparing tins

For most cakes it is necessary to line the tin with greaseproof paper, or non-stick baking parchment. Cakes that are particularly liable to stick, such as roulades and meringues, are best protected with baking parchment. If, in addition to greasing, a cake tin needs a coating of flour to prevent sticking, sprinkle a little flour into the lined and greased tin, tap and tilt to coat the base and sides evenly, then tip out excess.

Lining a round tin

Put the cake tin on a piece of greaseproof paper and draw around it. Cut out, just inside the line. Cut strip(s) of paper, about 2cm (¾in) wider than the depth of the tin. Fold up the bottom edge by 1cm (½in), then make cuts, 2.5cm (1in) apart, from the edge to the fold. Grease the tin. Position the paper strip(s) around the side of the tin so the snipped edge sits on the base. Lay the paper circle on top. Grease all the paper.

Lining a square tin

Cut a square of greaseproof paper fractionally smaller than the base of the tin. For the sides, cut strips about 2cm (¾in) wider than the depth of the tin. Fold up the bottom edge by 1cm (½in). Grease the tin. Make a cut from the edge of the paper to the fold and press into one corner. Continue fitting the paper around the cake tin, cutting it to fit at each corner. Lay the square of paper in the base, then grease all the paper.

Lining a Swiss roll tin/shallow baking tin

Grease the base and sides. Cut a rectangle of greaseproof paper, 7.5cm (3in) wider and longer than the tin. Press into the tin and cut the paper at the corners, then fold to fit. Grease the paper.

Lining a loaf tin

Grease the tin. Cut a greaseproof paper strip, the length of the base and wide enough to cover it and the long sides. Press into position. Cut another strip, the width of the tin base and long enough to cover the base and ends; position. Grease the paper.

Overwrapping a tin

This prevents the outside of a fruit cake overcooking. First line the inside, then cut a double thick strip of brown paper, the circumference of the tin and 2.5cm (1in) deeper. Wrap around the tin; tie with string.

Baking Techniques

The following step-by-step guides apply to many of the recipes.

Creaming method

1. Beat together the softened butter and sugar until pale and fluffy, and very light in consistency. Use an electric whisk, or beat vigorously with a wooden spoon.

2. Using an electric whisk or wooden spoon, beat in the eggs, a little at a time, beating well after each addition. To prevent curdling, a little of the measured flour can be added with the eggs.

3. Sift the flour over the creamed mixture, sifting high so that plenty of air is incorporated. Use a large metal spoon or spatula to gently fold in the flour, cutting and folding into the mixture using a figure-of-eight movement.

Cook's Tip: If the mixture is too firm to fold in the flour, add a dash of milk. Once the flour is incorporated the mixture should drop easily from the spoon when tapped against the side of the bowl.

Whisking Method

1. Put the eggs and sugar into a large heatproof bowl set over a pan of hot water. Whisk until the mixture is thick enough to leave a trail when the whisk is lifted from the bowl. Remove the bowl from the heat and continue whisking for about 5 minutes or until cool.

2. Sift half the flour over the mixture. Using a large metal spoon, gently cut and fold the flour into the whisked mixture. Sift the remaining flour on to the mixture and lightly fold in, until only just incorporated. Do not over-mix or the sponge mixture will reduce in volume.

Genoese Sponge

This is made by the whisking method, but melted butter is added with the flour. The butter must be cooled and beginning to thicken otherwise it will be difficult to incorporate.

Once half the flour has been folded into the whisked mixture, gradually pour in the cooled butter around the edge. Sift the remaining flour over the bowl and gently cut and fold it in as lightly as possible.

Creaming method

Whisking method

Turning Cake Mix into Tin

Turning Cake Mix into Tin

Spoon the mixture into the tin, dividing it evenly between the tins if making a sandwich cake. Use a palette knife to spread the cake mixture lightly and in an even layer, right to the edges.

Turning whisked sponge mixture into a tin

Pour the whisked mixture into the tin and tilt the tin so that the mixture spreads to the edges. If necessary, use a plastic spatula to gently spread it into the corners. Avoid over-spreading as this will crush the air bubbles.

Note: When mixing any type of cake, scrape down the sides of the bowl from time to time to ensure the ingredients are evenly incorporated.

Testing Baked Sponges

Carefully remove the cake from the oven and touch the centre with one hand. It should feel spongy and give very slightly. Whisked cakes should just be shrinking from the sides of the tin. If necessary, return the cake to the oven for a few minutes, closing the door very gently so that vibration does not cause the cake to sink in the centre.

Testing Fruit Cakes

Take the cake out of the oven, insert a skewer into the centre and remove: it should come away cleanly. If any mixture is sticking to the skewer, return the cake to the oven for a little longer.

Turning Out Cakes

Remove sponge cakes from the tins immediately after baking. Loosen the edges, then invert on to a wire cooling rack. If preferred, put a sheet of baking parchment dusted with sugar on the rack before inverting, to stop the soft sponge sticking to the rack. Semi-rich fruit cakes should be left to cool in the tin for about 15 minutes, while rich fruit cakes are left to cool completely in the tin as they tend to break up if removed while still warm.

Testing Baked Sponges

Turning Out Cakes

Melting Chocolate

Chocolate can be melted over a pan of gently simmering water, or in a microwave. Either way, you must avoid overheating, or water coming into contact with the chocolate, otherwise it is liable to become grainy, or 'seize' into a solid mass. Even condensation can cause the chocolate to seize. Particular care must be taken when melting white chocolate, which is very sensitive to heat.

To melt chocolate, break into pieces and put into a heatproof bowl set over a pan of gently simmering water, making sure that the bowl does not touch the water otherwise the chocolate will get too hot. Leave undisturbed until melted, then stir until smooth and remove the bowl from the pan.

To melt chocolate in a microwave, break into pieces, put into a bowl and microwave on High, allowing about 2 minutes for 125g (4oz) chocolate. It is safer to melt white or milk chocolate on a low setting, allowing about 4 minutes for 125g (4oz).

Melting chocolate

Pastry

For most pastries, plain flour works best, as it gives a light, crisp result. Puff pastry is usually made with strong flour as this contains extra gluten to strengthen the dough and Shortcrust pastry is made with a mixture of white vegetable fat and butter and margerine.

Shortcrust Pastry

This is the most widely used pastry. The proportion of flour to fat is 2:1. The choice of fat is largely a matter of taste – butter gives a rich pastry, but using half white vegetable fat improves the texture.

Hands-on time: 10 minutes, plus resting
Makes a 225g (8oz) quantity
per 25g (1oz): 110 cals, 6g fat, 12g carbohydrate

225g (8oz) plain flour, plus extra to dust
pinch of salt
110g (4oz) butter, or half white vegetable fat and
    half butter, cut into pieces

1. Sift the flour and salt into a bowl, add the fat and mix lightly.
2. Using your fingertips, rub the fat into the flour until the mixture resembles fine breadcrumbs.
3. Sprinkle 3–4 tbsp cold water evenly over the surface and stir with a round-bladed knife until the mixture begins to stick together in large lumps. If the dough seems dry, add a little extra water. With one hand, collect the dough together to form a ball.
4. Knead lightly on a lightly floured surface for a few seconds to form a smooth, firm dough; do not over-work. Wrap in clingfilm and leave to rest in the fridge for 30 minutes before rolling out.

Cook's Tips:
• To make the pastry in a food processor, put the flour and salt in the processor bowl with the butter. Whiz until the mixture resembles fine crumbs, then add the water. Process briefly, using the pulse button, until the mixture just comes together in a ball. Continue from stage 4.
• Shortcrust pastry can be stored in the fridge for up to 3 days, or frozen.

Puff Pastry

This is the richest of all pastries, and requires patience, practice and very light handling. If possible, it should be made the day before it is to be used. It is not practical to make less than a 450g (1lb) flour weight quantity.

Good quality ready-made puff pastry is available fresh and frozen, so use this for convenience if you prefer. Two 375g (13oz) packs would be roughly equivalent to this homemade quantity.

Hands-on time: 40 minutes, plus resting
Makes a 450g (1lb) quantity
Per 25g (1oz): 100 cals, 8g fat, 7g carbohydrate

450g (1lb) strong plain (bread) flour, plus
    extra to dust
pinch of salt
450g (1lb) butter, chilled
1 tbsp lemon juice

1. Sift the flour and salt together into a bowl. Cut off 50g (2oz) of the butter and flatten the remaining large block with a rolling pin to a slab, about 2cm (¾in) thick; set aside.
2. Cut the 50g (2oz) butter into small pieces and rub into the flour, using your fingertips.
3. Using a round-bladed knife, stir in the lemon juice and enough chilled water to make a soft elastic dough; you will need about 300ml (½ pint).
4. Turn out on to a lightly floured surface and quickly knead the dough until smooth. Cut a cross through half of the depth, then open out to form a star.
5. Roll out, keeping the centre four times as thick as the flaps. Put the slab of butter in the centre of the dough. Fold the flaps over the dough, envelope-style.
6. Press gently with a rolling pin and roll out to a rectangle, measuring 40 x 20cm (16 x 8in).

7. Fold the bottom third up and the top third down, keeping the edges straight. Wrap in clingfilm and leave to rest in the fridge for 30 minutes.
8. Put the pastry on a lightly floured surface with the folded edges to the sides. Repeat the rolling, folding, resting and turning sequence five times.
9. Shape the puff pastry as required, then rest in the fridge for about 30 minutes before baking.

Baking Blind

If a recipe instructs you to 'bake blind' you need to bake, or part-bake the pastry case without its filling. The pastry may be partially cooked before filling, or completely cooked if the filling does not require baking.

1. Prick the pastry base with a fork, to prevent air bubbles forming, then line with a large piece of greaseproof paper.
2. Fill the paper with a single layer of ceramic baking beans or dried pulses to weight the dough.
3. Bake the tart case at the temperature suggested in the recipe for 10–15 minutes or until the pastry looks set, then lift out the greaseproof paper and beans. Bake the tart case for a further 5 minutes until the base is firm to the touch and lightly coloured; or a further 15 minutes until crisp and golden brown if the pastry case requires complete baking.

Icings and Frostings

Icings and frostings are used to fill, cover and decorate cakes. Some icings are poured over the cake to give a smooth glossy finish, others need to be spread or swirled to give a textured finish. Fresh whipped cream and buttercream may be smoothed flat, textured with a palette knife, or piped. Sometimes the same mixture is used to fill and cover the cake, or it may be different – a jam-filled sponge, for example, can be topped with buttercream or glacé icing.

The filling must have the right consistency for spreading: if too firm it will pull the crumbs from the cake, making an untidy layer; if too soft it will cause the cake layers to slip and move around, and ooze out of the side of the cake. Use a palette knife dipped in hot water for spreading the filling. Jam should be warmed gently until thinned to a spreading consistency.

To cover a cake with buttercream or crème au beurre icing, use a small palette knife dipped in hot water to spread the icing smoothly and evenly. For a textured effect, paddle the palette knife backwards and forwards, or swirl the icing decoratively. For a more formal finish, pipe a design directly on to the surface of the cake, such as a piped scroll, shell or swirl edging.

Once a cake has been covered with icing or frosting, the sides may be coated with crushed praline, grated chocolate or toasted chopped or flaked nuts; pistachio nuts, in particular, add colour as well as texture. Simple finishing touches are often the most effective – a drizzle of melted chocolate or caramel, fresh or frosted herbs and flowers, fresh fruit, toasted nuts and chocolate curls all work well.

Glacé Icing

Hands-on time: 5 minutes
Makes 225g (8oz)
Per 25g (1oz): 100 cals, 0g fat, 26g carbohydrate

225g (8oz) icing sugar
few drops of vanilla extract (optional)
few drops of food colouring (optional)

1. Sift the icing sugar into a bowl. Add a few drops of vanilla extract if you like.
2. Using a wooden spoon, gradually stir in 2–3 tbsp hot water until the mixture is the

consistency of thick cream. Beat until white and smooth and the icing is thick enough to coat the back of the spoon. Add colouring if you like, and use straightaway.

Cook's Tip: This quantity is sufficient to cover the top of one large sandwich cake, or about 16 small cakes.

Variations
Orange or lemon glacé icing: Replace the water with strained orange or lemon juice.
Chocolate glacé icing: Sift 2tsp cocoa powder with the icing sugar.
Coffee glacé icing: Flavour the icing with 1tsp coffee essence or 2tsp instant coffee granules dissolved in 1tbsp of the hot water.

Buttercream
Hands-on time: 5 minutes
Makes 250g (9oz)
Per 25g (1oz): 130 cals, 6g fat (of which
   4g saturates), 18g carbohydrate

75g (3oz) unsalted butter, softened
175g (6oz) icing sugar, sifted
few drops of vanilla extract
1–2tbsp milk or water

1. Put the butter into a bowl and beat with a wooden spoon until it is light and fluffy.
2. Gradually stir in the icing sugar, vanilla extract and milk. Beat well until light and smooth.

Cook's Tip: This quantity is sufficient to cover the top of a 20cm (8in) cake. To make enough to cover the top and sides, increase the quantities by one third.

Variations
Orange, lime or lemon buttercream: Replace the vanilla extract with a little finely grated orange, lime or lemon zest. Add 1–2tbsp juice from the fruit instead of the milk, beating well to avoid curdling the mixture. If the mixture is to be piped, omit the zest.
Chocolate buttercream: Blend 1tbsp cocoa powder with 2tbsp boiling water and cool before adding to the mixture.

Coffee buttercream: Replace the vanilla extract with 2tsp instant coffee granules dissolved in 1tbsp boiling water; cool before adding to the mixture.

Crème au Beurre
Preparation: 15 minutes · Cooking time: 5 minutes
Makes 275g (10oz)
Per 25g (1oz): 160 cals, 9g fat, 7g carbohydrate

75g (3oz) golden caster sugar
2 medium egg yolks, beaten
175g (6oz) unsalted butter, softened

1. Put the caster sugar and 4tbsp water into a heavy-based pan and heat gently to dissolve the sugar, without boiling.
2. When the sugar has completely dissolved, bring to the boil and boil steadily for 2–3 minutes until the syrup registers 107°C on a sugar thermometer (i.e. the thread stage – when a little syrup placed between two dry teaspoons and pulled apart forms a fine thread).
3. Put the egg yolks into a bowl and pour on the syrup in a thin stream, whisking all the time with a hand-held electric whisk. Continue to whisk until the mixture is thick and cold.
4. In another bowl, cream the butter until light and fluffy. Gradually add the egg yolk mixture, whisking well after each addition.

Variations
Orange or lemon crème au beurre: Add the finely grated zest and a little orange or lemon juice to taste at stage 4.
Chocolate crème au beurre: Melt 50g (2oz) plain chocolate, cool slightly, then beat into the crème au beurre mixture at stage 4.
Coffee crème au beurre: Dissolve 1–2tbsp coffee granules in 1tbsp boiling water. Cool, then beat into the crème au beurre mixture at stage 4.

Almond Paste

Hands-on time: 10 minutes
Makes 450g (1lb)
Per 25g (1oz): 140 cals; 7g fat (of which trace saturates); 15g carbohydrate

225g (8oz) ground almonds
125g (4oz) golden caster sugar
125g (4oz) golden icing sugar
1 large egg
1tsp lemon juice
1tsp sherry
1–2 drops vanilla extract

1. Put the ground almonds, caster sugar and icing sugar into a bowl and mix together. In a separate bowl, whisk the egg with the remaining ingredients and add to the dry mixture.
2. Stir well to mix, pounding gently to release some of the oil from the almonds. Knead with your hands until smooth. Cover until ready to use.

Cook's Tip: If you wish to avoid using raw egg to bind the almond paste, mix the other liquid ingredients with a little water instead.

Royal Icing

Hands-on time: 20 minutes
Makes 450g (1lb)
Per 25g (1oz): 100 cals, 0g fat; 26g carbohydrate

2 large egg whites, or 1tbsp egg albumen powder
2tsp liquid glycerine (optional, see note)
450g (1lb) icing sugar, sifted

1. If using the egg whites and the glycerine, put them in a bowl and stir just enough to break up the egg whites. If using albumen powder, mix according to manufacturer's instructions.
2. Add a little icing sugar and mix gently with a wooden spoon to incorporate as little air as possible.
3. Add a little more icing sugar as the mixture becomes lighter. Continue to add the icing sugar, stirring gently but thoroughly until the mixture is stiff and stands in soft peaks. For coating it should form soft peaks; for piping it should be a little stiffer.

4. Transfer to an airtight container, cover the surface closely with clingfilm to prevent it drying out, then seal. When required, stir the icing slowly.

Cook's Tip: Glycerine keeps the icing from becoming hard. Omit it if the icing is required to cover a tiered cake, as a very hard surface is required to support the tiers.

SAUCES

Butterscotch Sauce

(see Spiced Apple Pastry page 102)
Cooking time: 10 minutes
Serves 8
240 cals, 15g fat (of which 9g saturates) 31g carbohydrate per serving

50g (2oz) butter
75g (3oz) light soft brown (muscovado) sugar
50g (2oz) caster sugar
150g (5oz) golden syrup
142ml carton double cream
few drops vanilla extract
juice of ½ lemon

1. In a medium-size saucepan slowly melt together the butter, sugars and syrup. Stir over a low heat for a further 5 minutes.
2. Off the heat, slowly add the cream. Add the vanilla extract and lemon juice and stir for 1–2 minutes. Serve hot or cold.

Ginger and Whisky Sauce

(see Warm Ginger Ricotta Cake, page 70)
Hands-on time: 2 minutes · Cooking time: 2 minutes
Serves 6–8
100–75 cals, 9–7g fat (of which 6–4g saturates), 2–2g carbohydrate per serving

284ml (10fl oz) carton single cream
2tsp stem-ginger syrup
2tsp whisky

1. Heat all the ingredients together without boiling. Serve just warm with the cake.

CLASSIC CAKES

All the old favourites can be found here. What could be more comforting and homely than a Victoria Sponge? Simple to make and delicious to taste, the classic recipes are the best. Dainty Cup Cakes are perfect with a cup of tea and the gooey Mississippi Pie is a great after dinner treat. Which is your preferred golden oldie? Try them all first before you decide.

Carrot Cake

Sticky Ginger Cake

Espresso Coffee Cake

Cinnamon Coffee Cake

Genoese Sponge

Sticky Almond Cake

Date and Ginger Cake

Sour Cherry Cakes

Dainty Cup Cakes

The Easiest Christmas Cake Ever

30-Minute Fruit Cake

Warm Lemon Syrup Cake

Victoria Sponge

Baklava

Mississippi Mud Pie

Carrot Cake

Hands-on time: 20 minutes · Cooking time: 30–40 minutes, plus cooling
Serves 12: 490 cals, 36g fat (of which 11g saturates), 38g carbohydrate per serving

butter to grease
250ml (9fl oz) sunflower oil
225g (8oz) light muscovado sugar
3 large eggs
225g (8oz) self-raising flour
large pinch of salt
½tsp each ground mixed spice, nutmeg and
    cinnamon
250g (9oz) carrots, coarsely grated

For the frosting
50g (2oz) unsalted butter, softened
225g (8oz) full-fat cream cheese
25g (1oz) golden icing sugar
½tsp vanilla extract

For the decoration
8 pecan halves, roughly chopped

1 Preheat the oven to 180°C (160°C fan oven) mark 4. Grease two 18cm (7in) sandwich tins and baseline with greaseproof paper.

2 Using a handheld electric mixer, whisk the sunflower oil and the muscovado sugar together to combine, then whisk in the eggs one at a time.

3 Sift the flour, salt and spices together into a bowl, then fold gently into the sugar and egg mixture with a large metal spoon. Tip the grated carrots into the bowl and fold again to mix well.

4 Divide the mixture between the cake tins and bake for 30–40 minutes until golden and a skewer inserted into the centre comes out clean. Leave in the tins for 10 minutes, then turn out on to a wire rack to cool.

5 For the frosting, beat together the butter and cream cheese until light and fluffy. Sift in the icing sugar, add the vanilla extract and mix well until all the ingredients are thoroughly combined.

6 Remove the lining paper from the cakes when cold. Spread one-third of the frosting over one cake and put the other cake on top. Spread the remaining frosting over the cake, then sprinkle with pecans (see picture on page 1).

Sticky Ginger Cake

Hands-on time: 20 minutes · Cooking time: 35 minutes, plus cooling

Serves 15: 260 cals, 11g fat (of which 6g saturates), 39g carbohydrate per serving

175g (6oz) butter, diced, plus extra to
  grease
150g (5oz) dark muscovado sugar
3tbsp black treacle
150ml (5fl oz) semi-skimmed milk
2 balls of stem ginger, grated
225g (8oz) plain flour, sifted
1tbsp ground ginger

1½tsp ground cinnamon
1½tsp bicarbonate of soda
2 medium eggs, beaten

For the icing
150g (5oz) golden icing sugar
2tbsp ginger syrup from the jar
1 ball of stem ginger, roughly chopped

1 Preheat the oven to 200°C (180°C fan oven) mark 6. Grease a 20.5cm (8in) square cake tin and baseline with greaseproof paper.

2 Put the butter, muscovado sugar, treacle, milk and grated ginger in a large pan and heat gently until melted, stirring to mix well.

3 Add the flour, spices and bicarbonate of soda, then add the beaten eggs. Quickly mix together, then spoon into the prepared tin. Bake for 30 minutes. Remove from the tin and cool, still in the paper, on a wire rack.

4 For the icing, sift the icing sugar into a bowl, add the syrup and 1tbsp cold water, then mix. When the cake has cooled, pour the icing over, then scatter with the chopped ginger.

Espresso Coffee Cake

Hands-on time: 30 minutes · Cooking time: 45–50 minutes, plus cooling

Serves 12: 310 cals, 14g fat (of which 8g saturates), 44g carbohydrate per serving

175g (6oz) unsalted butter, softened, plus extra to grease
175g (6oz) golden caster sugar
3 medium eggs
175g (6oz) self-raising flour, sifted
1tsp baking powder
1tbsp coffee-flavour liqueur, such as Tia Maria

3tbsp instant espresso coffee, dissolved in 1tbsp boiling water

For the icing
175g (6oz) golden icing sugar, sifted
2tsp instant espresso coffee, dissolved in 2tbsp and 1tsp boiling water
18 dark chocolate-covered coffee beans, roughly chopped

1 Preheat the oven to 190°C (170°C fan oven) mark 5. Grease a 900g (2lb) loaf tin and line with greaseproof paper.

2 To make the cake, put the butter and caster sugar into the bowl of a freestanding mixer and cream together until the mixture becomes pale and fluffy. Beat in the eggs, one at a time, adding 1tbsp flour if the mixture looks like it's starting to curdle.

3 Sift the remaining flour and the baking powder into the bowl, add the coffee liqueur and fold everything together. Put half the mixture into another bowl and mix in the coffee.

4 Spoon a dollop of each mixture into the prepared tin, then repeat with the remaining mixture to create two layers. Shake the tin once to distribute the mixture, then swirl a skewer backwards and forwards through it three times to create a marbled effect. Bake for 45–50 minutes or until a skewer inserted into the centre comes out clean. Turn out on to a wire rack and leave to cool.

5 To make the icing, put the golden icing sugar in a bowl, add the coffee and stir together. Pour over the top of the cake and decorate with the coffee beans.

Cinnamon Coffee Cake

Hands-on time: 15 minutes · Cooking time: 35–40 minutes

Serves 8: 470 cals, 31g fat (of which 12g saturates), 42g carbohydrate per serving

125g (4oz) unsalted butter, plus extra to
    grease
200g (7oz) granulated sugar
2 medium eggs
142ml carton soured cream
2tsp vanilla extract

125g (4oz) plain flour, plus extra to dust
2tsp baking powder
pinch of salt
150g (5oz) walnuts or pecan nuts, chopped
2tsp ground cinnamon

1 Preheat the oven to 180°C (160°C fan oven) mark 4. Grease a deep 20.5cm (8in) round cake tin and baseline with greaseproof paper. Lightly dust with flour.

2 Cream together the butter and 175g (6oz) of the sugar. Beat in the eggs, soured cream and vanilla extract. Sift the flour, baking powder and salt into the mixture and fold in. Do not overbeat.

3 Mix the remaining sugar with the nuts and cinnamon.

4 Spoon half the cake mixture into the prepared tin. Sprinkle over half the nut mixture. Add the remaining cake mixture and top with the rest of the nut mixture.

5 Bake for 35–40 minutes. Serve warm or cold with coffee.

Genoese Sponge

Hands-on time: 25 minutes · Cooking time: 25–40 minutes

Serves 6–8: 190–140 cals, 9–8g fat (of which 4–3g saturates), 24–18g carbohydrate per serving

40g (1½oz) unsalted butter, plus extra to
   grease
65g (2½oz) plain flour, plus extra to dust
75g (3oz) golden caster sugar, plus extra
   to dust
3 large eggs
1 tbsp cornflour

To assemble
soft fruit and whipped cream, or jam
icing sugar, to dust

1 Preheat the oven to 180°C (160°C fan oven) mark 4. Grease two 18cm (7in) sandwich tins, or one deep 18cm (7in) round cake tin and baseline with greaseproof paper, then dust with a little flour and caster sugar.

2 Put the butter into a pan and heat gently until melted, then remove from the heat and leave to cool slightly for a few minutes until beginning to thicken.

3 Put the eggs and caster sugar into a large heatproof bowl and whisk until evenly blended, using an electric whisk. Put the bowl over a pan of hot water and whisk until pale and thick enough to leave a trail on the surface when the whisk is lifted. Remove the bowl from the pan and whisk until cool and thick.

4 Sift the flour and cornflour together. Fold half into the whisked mixture with a large metal spoon or plastic spatula. Pour the cooled butter around the edge of the mixture, leaving the sediment behind. Gradually fold it in very lightly, cutting through the mixture until it is all incorporated. Carefully fold in the remaining flour as lightly as possible. Pour into the prepared tins.

5 Bake for 25–30 minutes, or the deep cake for 35–40 minutes, until well risen and the cakes spring back when lightly pressed. Loosen the cake edge and leave in the tins for 5 minutes.

6 Upturn on to wire racks, remove the lining paper and leave to cool. Mix together the fruit and cream, or jam, and use to sandwich the cake together. Dust with icing sugar.

Sticky Almond Cake

Hands-on time: 20 minutes · Cooking time: 1¼ hours, plus chilling
Serves 10: 550 cals, 35g fat (of which 13g saturates), 54g carbohydrate per serving

225g (8oz) unsalted butter, plus extra to
    grease
225g (8oz) caster sugar
4 medium eggs, beaten
50g (2oz) plain flour, sifted

175g (6oz) ground almonds
½tsp almond extract
350g (12oz) white marzipan
icing sugar to dust

1 Preheat the oven to 180°C (160°C fan oven) mark 4. Grease a 21.5cm-23cm (8½-9in) spring-release cake tin and baseline with greaseproof paper.

2 Cream together the butter and caster sugar until very pale. Gradually beat in the eggs, adding a little flour if the mixture curdles. Stir in the remaining flour, then gently fold in the ground almonds and extract.

3 Roll out the marzipan slightly larger than the cake tin. Using the tin as a template, cut the marzipan into a circle.

4 Spoon half the cake mixture into the prepared tin. Top with the marzipan, then finish with cake mixture.

5 Bake for about 1¼ hours or until firm to the touch, covering lightly with foil if needed. Cool for 5 minutes in the tin, then remove and cool on a wire rack. Wrap in foil and store for at least one day before serving. Dust with icing sugar.

Date and Ginger Cake

Hands-on time: 20 minutes · Cooking time: around 1 hour

Serves 16: 220 cals, 7g fat (of which 4g saturates), 38g carbohydrate per serving

½tsp bicarbonate of soda
50ml (2fl oz) milk
125g (4oz) unsalted butter
125g (4oz) light muscovado sugar
2 medium eggs, beaten
150g (5oz) golden syrup
150g (5oz) black treacle

125g (4oz) stoned dates, roughly chopped
50g (2oz) stem ginger in syrup, roughly chopped
225g (8oz) plain flour, sifted
1½tsp ground ginger
pinch of salt

1 Preheat the oven to 150°C (130°C fan oven) mark 2. Grease a 23cm (9in) square cake tin and line with greaseproof paper. Stir the bicarbonate of soda into the milk.

2 Beat together the butter and sugar until pale and light. Slowly add the beaten eggs and then stir in the syrup, treacle, milk, chopped dates and stem ginger. Fold in the flour, ground ginger and salt. Pour the mixture into the prepared tin and bake for 1 hour or until a skewer inserted into the centre comes out clean. Leave in the tin for 1 hour. Turn out on to a wire rack to cool.

Sour Cherry Cakes

Hands-on time: 30 minutes · Cooking time: 15–20 minutes

Serves 12: 330 cals, 14g fat (of which 8g saturates), 51g carbohydrate per serving

175g (6oz) unsalted butter, softened
175g (6oz) golden caster sugar
3 medium eggs
175g (6oz) self-raising flour, sifted

75g packet dried cherries
2tbsp milk
225g (8oz) golden icing sugar, sifted
3tbsp lemon juice, strained

1 Preheat the oven to 190°C (170°C fan oven) mark 5. Line a muffin tin with 12 muffin cases.

2 Put the butter and caster sugar in a bowl and cream together until pale, light and fluffy. Beat in the eggs, one at a time, folding in 1tbsp flour if the mixture looks like it's starting to curdle.

3 Put 12 dried cherries to one side. Fold the remaining flour, cherries and the milk into the creamed mixture until evenly combined. Spoon the mixture into the cases and bake for 15–20 minutes until pale golden and risen. Remove from the tin and cool on a wire rack.

4 Put the icing sugar in a bowl and mix with the lemon juice to make a smooth dropping consistency. Spoon on to the cakes and decorate each with a cherry.

Dainty Cup Cakes

Hands-on time: 15 minutes · Cooking time: 15-20 minutes
Serves 12: 320 cals, 14g fat (of which 8g saturates), 48g carbohydrate per serving

175g (6oz) unsalted butter, softened
175g (6oz) golden caster sugar
3 medium eggs
175g (6oz) self-raising flour, sifted
zest and juice of 1 lemon

For the frosted flowers
1 egg white

6 edible flowers, such as violas
caster sugar to dust

For the icing
225g (8oz) icing sugar, sifted
1 drop violet food colouring
2–3tbsp lemon juice, strained

1 Preheat the oven to 190°C (170°C fan oven) mark 5. Line a muffin tin with 12 muffin cases.

2 Put the butter and caster sugar in a bowl and cream together until pale, light and fluffy. Add the eggs, one at a time, and beat together, folding in 1tbsp flour if the mixture looks as if it's going to curdle. Then fold in the flour, lemon zest and juice and mix everything well.

3 Spoon the mixture into the cases and bake for 15–20 minutes until pale golden, risen and springy to touch. Cool on a wire rack.

4 To make the flowers, whisk the egg white in a clean bowl for 30 seconds until frothy. Brush the white over the flower petals and put on a wire rack resting on a piece of greaseproof paper. Dust heavily with caster sugar, then leave the flowers to dry.

5 To make the icing, put the icing sugar into a bowl with the violet food colouring. Mix in the lemon juice to create a smooth dropping consistency. Spoon the icing on to the cakes. Decorate with the frosted flowers and serve when the icing is completely set.

The Easiest Christmas Cake Ever

Hands-on time: 30 minutes · Cooking time: 2-2¾ hours
Serves 16: 420 calories 11g fat (of which 6g saturates), 74g carbohydrate per serving

1kg (2lb 4oz) mixed dried fruit
100g (3½oz) ready-to-eat pitted prunes, roughly chopped
50g (2oz) dried, ready-to-eat figs, roughly chopped
100g (3½oz) dried cranberries
2 balls of stem ginger in syrup, grated and syrup reserved
zest and juice of 1 orange

175ml (6fl oz) brandy
2 splashes Angostura bitters
175g (6oz) unsalted butter, cubed, plus extra to grease
175g (6oz) dark muscovado sugar
200g (7oz) self-raising flour, sifted
½tsp each ground cinnamon, freshly grated nutmeg and ground cloves
4 medium eggs, beaten

1 Preheat the oven to 150°C (130°C fan oven) mark 2. Grease a deep 20.5cm (8in) round cake tin and line the base and sides with greaseproof paper.

2 Put all the dried fruit in a very large pan and add the grated stem ginger, 1tbsp reserved ginger syrup, orange zest and juice, brandy and Angostura bitters. Bring to the boil, then simmer for 5 minutes. Add the butter and sugar and heat gently to melt. Stir occasionally to dissolve the sugar.

3 Take the pan off the heat and leave to cool for a couple of minutes. Add the flour, spices and beaten eggs, then mix together well.

4 Pour the mixture into the prepared tin and level the top. Wrap the sides of the tin in brown paper and secure with string to prevent the edge of the cake from over-baking. Bake for 2–2½ hours.

5 Leave in the tin for 2–3 hours, then remove and allow to cool on a wire rack, leaving the greaseproof paper on. Wrap the cake in a layer of clingfilm, then foil. Store in an airtight container.

COOK'S TIP: About 5 days before Christmas cover the top and sides of the cake with almond paste. Leave the cake to dry for a day or two before applying royal icing. See page 17 for icing recipes.

30-Minute Fruit Cake

Hands-on time: 15 minutes · Cooking time: 30 minutes

Serves 18: 180 cals, 9g fat (of which 5g saturates), 24g carbohydrate per serving

125g (4oz) unsalted butter, softened
125g (4oz) light muscovado sugar
grated zest of 1 lemon
2 medium eggs
few drops vanilla extract
150g (5oz) self-raising flour, sifted

1tsp baking powder
50g (2oz) glacé cherries, chopped
175g (6oz) mixed dried fruit
25g (1oz) desiccated coconut
25g (1oz) demerara sugar
50g (2oz) flaked almonds

1 Preheat the oven to 190°C (170°C fan oven) mark 5. Grease a shallow, 28 × 18cm (11 × 7in) oblong baking tin and baseline with greaseproof paper.

2 Beat together the butter, sugar, lemon zest, eggs, vanilla extract, flour and baking powder. Add a little lemon juice, if necessary, to form a soft dropping consistency. Stir in the cherries, dried fruit and coconut.

3 Spoon the mixture into the prepared tin, level the surface and sprinkle with demerara sugar and almonds. Bake for 30 minutes, or until golden.

4 Cool in the tin for a few minutes, then turn out on to a wire rack to cool.

Warm Lemon Syrup Cake

Hands-on time: 15 minutes · Cooking time: 1 hour

Serves 12: 360 cals, 18g fat (of which 10g saturates), 49g carbohydrate per serving

65g (2½oz) candied lemon peel (optional)
225g (8oz) unsalted butter, softened, plus
    extra to grease
zest of 2 lemons and 2tbsp lemon juice
225g (8oz) caster sugar
4 large eggs, beaten
225g (8oz) self-raising flour, sifted

For the syrup
175g (6oz) caster sugar
juice of 3 lemons, strained
75ml (3fl oz) water

1 Preheat the oven to 180°C (160°C fan oven) mark 4. Grease and baseline a 21.5cm (8½in) base measurement moule à manqué tin with greaseproof paper. (This is a deep cake tin with sloping sides; if unavailable, use a deep round cake tin of a similar size.) Finely chop the candied peel, if using.

2 For the cake, cream together the butter and lemon zest. Gradually beat in the caster sugar, followed by the eggs, keeping the mixture stiff. Lastly, fold in the flour, candied peel, if using, and lemon juice. Spoon the mixture into the prepared tin and bake for about 1 hour, or until golden.

3 Meanwhile, prepare the syrup. Put the sugar, lemon juice and water in a pan. Warm gently until the sugar dissolves, then bring to the boil and bubble for 1 minute. Cool.

4 As soon as the cake is cooked, turn out on to an edged dish and immediately spoon over the syrup. Leave for about 30 minutes for the syrup to soak in. Serve warm with poached fruit.

Victoria Sponge

Hands-on time: 30 minutes · Cooking time: 25–30 minutes

Serves 12: 540 cals, 27g fat (of which 16g saturates), 72g carbohydrate per serving

250g (9oz) unsalted butter, softened, plus
    extra to grease
250g (9oz) golden caster sugar
5 medium eggs
250g (9oz) self-raising flour

For the filling
200g (7oz) mascarpone cheese
7tbsp strawberry conserve

For the decoration
250g (9oz) white icing sugar
few drops pink food colouring
1tsp rosewater

1 Preheat the oven to 190°C (170°C fan oven) mark 5. Grease two 20.5 × 4.5cm (8 × 1¾in) sandwich tins and baseline with greaseproof paper.

2 Put the butter and caster sugar in a large bowl and cream together using a handheld electric whisk until the mixture is pale, light and fluffy. Add three of the eggs, one at a time, whisking well between each addition.

3 Add 4tbsp of the flour (to stop the mixture curdling), then whisk in the remaining eggs, one at a time, and continue to whisk. Sift the remaining flour into the bowl and fold gently into the mixture using a large spoon. The mixture should be smooth and have a dropping consistency.

4 Divide the mixture between the prepared tins and level the top. Bake for 25–30 minutes until golden, springy to touch and shrinking away from the sides of the tins.

5 Leave to cool in the tins for 5 minutes, then turn on to a wire rack and remove the lining paper. When cold, spread one cake with mascarpone. Spoon on the jam, then spread to the edges. Top with the other cake and press down lightly.

6 Sift the icing sugar into a bowl, then add the pink food colouring, rosewater and 2–2½tbsp hot water to create a smooth dropping consistency. Pour the icing on top of the cake, spreading it to the edge so it drizzles down the side.

COOK'S TIP: Handheld electric whisks achieve the deepest, lightest sponge cakes – far better than using a large freestanding mixer. Food processors are fine to use for all-in-one sponge cakes when you're really short of time, although the cake will never be quite as light and airy.

Baklava

Hands-on time: 45 minutes, plus soaking · Cooking time: 30 minutes
Serves 8: 500 cals, 36g fat (of which 10g saturates), 36g carbohydrate per serving

For the baklava
125g (4oz) almonds with skins
50g (2oz) shelled pistachio nuts
125g (4oz) walnuts
75g (3oz) light muscovado sugar
1tsp ground cinnamon
pinch of ground cloves

8 sheets filo pastry, approx 19 × 38cm
    (7½ × 15in), about 200g (7oz) total weight
125g (4oz) unsalted butter, melted

For the syrup
6tbsp runny honey
4tbsp cold water
2tbsp lemon juice
few drops orange flower water (optional)

1 Preheat the oven to 200°C (180°C fan oven) mark 6. Place the almonds and pistachio nuts in separate heatproof bowls, cover with boiling water and leave for about 2 minutes. Strain and remove the skins. Toast the almonds and walnuts; leave to cool. Whiz one-third of all the nuts in a food processor until finely chopped; mix in the sugar and spices. Roughly chop the remaining nuts.

2 Cut each filo pastry sheet into three to produce 24 rectangles measuring 12.5 × 19cm (5 × 7½in). Keep covered with a slightly damp teatowel to prevent them from drying out. Grease a baking sheet, place one piece of filo pastry on the sheet, brush gently with melted butter and place another piece of filo on top. Butter again, then sprinkle over about 2tbsp of the ground nut mixture, followed by some of the chopped nuts. Top with two more pieces of filo, butter in between and again on top. Continue layering up with the nut mixtures and pastry until you have three layers of nut filling, finishing with two sheets of pastry. Lightly butter the top.

3 Grease another baking sheet and repeat step 2 twice more, making three separate 'mini' baklavas. Score one of the baklavas on the top with a knife to make a diamond pattern. Bake all three pastries for 15 minutes, then reduce the oven temperature to 180°C (160°C fan oven) mark 4 and bake for a further 10–15 minutes, until crisp and golden. Remove from the oven.

4 Meanwhile, prepare the syrup. Place the honey and cold water in a small pan. Bring to the boil and bubble for 1–2 minutes, until slightly thickened. Stir in the lemon juice and orange flower water, if using. Trim the edges of each pastry to neaten. Spoon the syrup evenly over each rectangle and leave to soak, basting occasionally, for about 30 minutes.

5 Transfer one pastry rectangle onto a wire rack over a baking sheet. Stack the others on top, scored one uppermost. Spoon over the remaining syrup, until all the liquid is soaked up. Leave to stand for an hour before serving with whipped cream or yogurt.

Mississippi Mud Pie

Hands-on time: 1 hour, plus chilling · Cooking time: 30-40 minutes

Serves 16: 610 cals, 43g fat (of which 23g saturates), 55g carbohydrate per serving

For the base
oil to grease
50g (2oz) unsalted butter
75g (3oz) digestive biscuits, crushed
75g (3oz) ginger biscuits, crushed

For the filling
600ml (1 pint) double cream
450g (1lb) caster sugar
4tbsp cornflour
4 large eggs, beaten

100g (3½oz) unsalted butter, cubed
1tsp vanilla extract
2tbsp rum
2tsp instant coffee, dissolved in 2tsp boiling
    water

For the topping
100g (3½oz) plain chocolate, broken up
2 large eggs, separated
150ml (5fl oz) double cream

1 To make the base, lightly oil a deep 20.5cm (8in) spring-release cake tin and line the base and sides with non-stick baking parchment. Melt the butter and leave to cool slightly. Stir the biscuits into the butter until combined. Press the mixture over the base of the tin and chill for 30 minutes.

2 To make the filling, place the cream and sugar in a heavy-based pan and heat gently, stirring occasionally, until the sugar has completely dissolved – at least 5 minutes. Remove from the heat. Mix the cornflour to a smooth paste with 4tbsp cold water. Stir the cornflour and beaten eggs into the cream and sugar mixture and beat well until thoroughly combined. Return to the heat and bring to the boil – stirring constantly with a wooden spoon – until the mixture becomes very thick and smooth like fudge. This will take 15–20 minutes. (The mixture will stick to the pan unless stirred constantly.) Beat the butter into the fudge mixture, a little at a time, with all the remaining filling ingredients until well combined. Pour the filling over the chilled biscuit base. Allow to cool completely, then place in the freezer for at least 1 hour to set, preferably overnight.

3 To make the topping, melt the chocolate (see page 13). Whisk the egg yolks and cream together and pour over the melted chocolate, whisking until smooth. Place in a small, heavy-based pan over a low heat and stir until smooth and thickly coating the back of a wooden spoon. Do not boil. Press a damp piece of greaseproof paper on to the surface and leave to cool.

4 When the mixture is cool, whisk the egg whites until just peaking. Stir about one-third into the chocolate mixture, then gently fold in the remainder. Pour over the set fudge filling and chill for at least 2–3 hours before serving.

CHOCOLATE CAKES

Chocolate, chocolate and more chocolate – these cakes don't hold back! You'll find lashings of chocolate and ganache galore for every occasion. If you're baking someone a special cake, try The Best Chocolate Cake in the World – rich, delicious and impressive, or indulge in the heavenly goo of the White Chocolate Mousse Cake.

Orange and White Chocolate Cake

Chocolate Cup Cakes

The Best Chocolate Cake in the World

Chocolate Temptation

Devil's Food Cake

Refrigerator Cake

Hazelnut and Chocolate Meringue Cake

Chocolate and Chestnut Roulade

The Ultimate Chocolate Cake

Decadent Chocolate Cake

Rich Chocolate Log

Viennese Chocolate Cake

Chocolate and Orange Marble Cake

White Chocolate Mousse Cake

Cherry Chocolate Pudding

Chocolate and Cherry Cups

Orange and White Chocolate Cake

Hands-on time: 35 minutes · Cooking time: 40 minutes, plus chilling
Serves 14: 550 cals, 36g fat (of which 16g saturates), 49g carbohydrate per serving

butter to grease
6 large eggs, separated
250g (9oz) golden caster sugar
150g (5oz) each self-raising flour, sifted
    and ground almonds
zest of 2 oranges

For the syrup
100g (3½oz) golden granulated sugar
225ml (8fl oz) sweet white wine
juice of 3 large oranges

For the white chocolate ganache
225g (8oz) white chocolate, chopped
568ml carton double cream
350g (12oz) strawberries, thinly sliced

1 Preheat the oven to 180°C (160°C fan oven) mark 4. Grease a deep 23cm (9in) round cake tin and line with greaseproof paper.

2 Put the egg whites in a bowl and whisk until they form soft peaks. Gradually beat in 50g (2oz) caster sugar. Whisk until the mixture stands in stiff peaks and looks glossy. Put the egg yolks and remaining sugar in another bowl. Whisk until soft and moussey. Carefully stir in the flour to make a paste. Fold a third of the egg whites into the paste, then fold in the remaining egg whites, ground almonds and orange zest.

3 Pour the mixture into the prepared tin and bake for 35 minutes or until a skewer inserted into the centre comes out clean. Cool in the tin for 10 minutes, then turn out on to a wire rack to cool.

4 Put the syrup ingredients in a small pan and stir over a gentle heat until the sugar has dissolved. Bring to the boil and bubble for 5 minutes or until syrupy. Cool and set aside.

5 To make the ganache, put the chocolate in a heatproof bowl with half the cream. Melt over a pan of simmering water, then stir to combine. Cool, then beat with a wooden spoon until cold and thick. Whip the remaining cream lightly and beat a large spoonful into the chocolate cream to loosen it. Fold in the remainder. Chill for 2 hours.

6 Cut the cake in half horizontally, pierce all over with a skewer and put it, cut sides up, on an edged tray or baking sheet. Spoon over the syrup and leave to soak in. Spread a quarter of the ganache over the base cake and scatter with 225g (8oz) strawberries. Cover with the top half of the cake and press down lightly. Using a palette knife, smooth the remaining ganache over the top and sides of the cake. Chill for up to 4 hours. Decorate with the remaining strawberries and serve.

Chocolate Cup Cakes

Hands-on time: 15 minutes · Cooking time: 20 minutes, plus cooling and setting
Serves 18: 260 cals, 16g fat (of which 9g saturates), 29g carbohydrate per serving

125g (4oz) unsalted butter, softened
125g (4oz) light muscovado sugar
2 medium eggs, beaten
15g (½oz) cocoa powder, sifted
100g (3½oz) self-raising flour, sifted
100g (3½oz) dark chocolate (minimum 70% cocoa solids), roughly chopped

For the topping
142ml carton double cream
100g (3½oz) dark chocolate (minimum 70% cocoa solids), broken up

1 Preheat the oven to 190°C (170°C fan oven) mark 5. Line muffin tins with 18 muffin cases.

2 Beat together the butter and sugar until light and fluffy. Gradually beat in the eggs. Sift the cocoa powder with the flour and fold into the creamed mixture with the chopped chocolate.

3 Divide the mixture among the paper cases and lightly flatten the surface with the back of a spoon. Bake for 20 minutes. Cool in the cases.

4 For the topping, put the cream and broken up chocolate into a heavy-based pan and heat until melted, then allow to cool and thicken slightly. Pour over the cooled cakes and leave to set for 30 minutes.

The Best Chocolate Cake in the World

Hands-on time: 20 minutes · Cooking time: 1¼ hours, plus cooling and setting

Serves 16: 310 cals, 20g fat (of which 11g saturates), 29g carbohydrate per serving

200g (7oz) plain chocolate
125g (4oz) unsalted butter, cubed, plus
   extra to grease
8 medium eggs, separated
200g (7oz) golden caster sugar

For the chocolat and ganache
200g (7oz) plain chocolate
75ml (3fl oz) double cream
25g (1oz) unsalted butter

1 Preheat the oven to 180°C (160°C fan oven) mark 4. Grease a 23cm (9in) spring-release cake tin and line with greaseproof paper.

2 To make the cake, melt the chocolate with the butter (see page 13). Remove from the heat and cool for a few minutes.

3 Whisk the egg yolks and sugar in a bowl until pale and moussey, then whisk in the chocolate mixture. Whisk the egg whites until soft peaks form. Add a third of this to the chocolate mixture and fold in, using a large metal spoon. Add the remaining egg whites and mix everything together, then pour into the prepared tin and bake for 1¼ hours. Turn off the oven. Cover the cake with a damp teatowel and leave in the oven until the cake cools and the centre has sunk.

4 Meanwhile, to make the chocolate curls, melt half the chocolate and pour into a small rectangular container (a 250g margarine tub is perfect). Leave to cool so the chocolate hardens.

5 To make the ganache, melt the remaining chocolate with the cream and butter and stir until smooth. Take the cake out of the tin and peel off the paper. Spoon the ganache over the cake so it covers the top and drizzles down the sides. Leave until just set.

6 Push the set chocolate block out of the container and use a very sharp knife or vegetable peeler to make curls. Scatter the chocolate curls on top of the cake.

Chocolate Temptation

Hands-on time: 50 minutes, plus chilling · Cooking time: 1¼ hours
Serves 8: 800 cals, 52g fat (of which 29g saturates), 71g carbohydrate per serving

225g (8oz) plain chocolate, broken up
5 medium eggs, separated
150g (5oz) caster sugar
125g (4oz) unsalted butter, softened, plus
    extra to grease
4tbsp orange-flavour liqueur, such as
    Cointreau

For the mousse
142ml carton double cream
225g (8oz) plain chocolate
4 medium eggs, separated

To complete
cocoa powder to dust

1 Preheat the oven to 180°C (160°C fan oven) mark 4. Grease a 20.5cm (8in) spring-release cake tin and line the base and sides with greaseproof paper. Melt the broken-up chocolate (see page 13). Turn off the heat, but leave the bowl over the pan to keep the chocolate liquid.

2 Put the egg yolks and sugar in a heatproof bowl set over a pan of hot water (do not allow the bowl to come into contact with the water). Whisk for about 3 minutes or until thick and creamy. Continue whisking, adding the butter a little at a time, then lower the whisk setting to slow and whisk in the melted chocolate.

3 Whisk the egg whites until peaking, then fold into the chocolate mixture. Turn into the prepared tin and bake for 50 minutes or until risen and the top is beginning to crack. Leave to cool in the tin for 1 hour – the cake will sink but don't worry. Remove from the tin and slice it in half horizontally. Put the top piece, cut side up, back in the tin and drizzle over half the liqueur. Drizzle the remaining liqueur over the bottom half and set aside.

4 To make the mousse, lightly whip the cream and set aside. Melt the chocolate and allow to cool a little, then beat in the egg yolks. Fold in the whipped cream. Whisk the egg whites until peaking, then fold into the chocolate mixture. Spoon over the cake half in the tin, spreading it to the edges. Chill for 3 hours or overnight.

5 Top with the remaining cake half, cut side down. Remove the cake carefully from the tin and smooth the edges with a round-bladed knife. Serve dusted with cocoa powder.

Devil's Food Cake

Hands-on time: 30 minutes · Cooking time: 35 minutes, plus cooling

Serves 12: 430 cals, 21g fat (of which 12g saturates), 58g carbohydrate per serving

100g (3½oz) unsalted butter, softened,
    plus extra to grease
225ml (8fl oz) milk
1tbsp lemon juice
225g (8oz) plain flour
1tsp bicarbonate of soda
50g (2oz) cocoa powder
250g (9oz) golden caster sugar
3 medium eggs, beaten

For the soured cream frosting
250g (9oz) plain chocolate, broken into small
    pieces
3tbsp golden caster sugar
2 × 142ml cartons soured cream

1 Preheat the oven to 180°C (160°C fan oven) mark 4. Grease two 20.5cm (8in) sandwich tins and baseline with greaseproof paper.

2 Pour the milk into a jug, then add the lemon juice or vinegar and leave for 5 minutes. Sift the flour, bicarbonate of soda and cocoa powder together.

3 In a large bowl, cream the butter with half the sugar until light. Gradually beat in the eggs, then mix in the rest of the sugar. Add the reserved soured milk alternately with the flour mixture – around a couple of tablespoons at a time.

4 Divide the mixture between the prepared tins and level the tops. Bake in the oven for 30 minutes. Leave in the tins for 10 minutes, then turn out on to a wire rack to cool.

5 For the frosting, melt the chocolate (see page 13), then whisk in the sugar and soured cream.

6 Slice each cake in half to make four discs. Put one base on a plate and spread with a quarter of the frosting. Repeat until the cake is layered up, then finish with a layer of frosting on the top.

Refrigerator Cake

Hands-on time: 10–15 minutes · Cooking time: 5–10 minutes, plus soaking and chilling
Serves 12: 410 cals, 22g fat (of which 12g saturates), 47g carbohydrate per serving

150g (5oz) dried apricots, chopped
150g (5oz) ready-to-eat prunes, roughly
  chopped
3 large balls of stem ginger, drained and
  chopped
1½tbsp ginger syrup from the jar
75g (3oz) golden syrup

125ml (4fl oz) brandy
little oil to grease
350g (12oz) plain chocolate, broken into
  pieces
150g (5oz) unsalted butter
175g (6oz) digestive biscuits, crushed

1 Put the apricots, prunes, stem ginger and syrup, golden syrup and brandy into a pan. Bring to the boil and simmer for 2–3 minutes, then remove from the heat and leave the fruit to soak in the syrup for 30 minutes. Lightly oil an 18cm (7in) square cake tin, then line it with clingfilm, leaving enough hanging over the rim to wrap up the cake entirely.

2 Meanwhile, melt the chocolate and butter (see page 13). When both have melted, stir until mixed together.

3 Add the biscuits and soaked fruit to the bowl and mix all the ingredients together. Spoon the mixture into the prepared tin, tapping it once or twice to allow the mixture to settle, then level the surface. Seal up in the clingfilm and chill for at least 6 hours or overnight.

4 To serve, turn the cake on to a board and peel off the clingfilm. Cut into thick slices.

Hazelnut and Chocolate Meringue Cake

Hands-on time: 15 minutes · Cooking time: 1½ hours, plus cooling and chilling

Serves 10: 500 cals, 39g fat (of which 16g saturates), 34g carbohydrate per serving

175g (6oz) hazelnuts

For the meringue
4 egg whites
100g (3½oz) caster sugar
100g (3½oz) light muscovado sugar

For the icing
125g (4oz) plain chocolate
450ml (15fl oz) double cream
icing sugar to decorate

1 Preheat the oven to 150°C (130°C fan oven) mark 2. Toast the hazelnuts until well browned, rub off their skins and cool. Finely chop 125g (4oz) of the nuts and grind the remainder. Line two baking sheets with non-stick baking parchment and draw a 20.5cm (8in) circle on each. Turn the paper over so the pencil mark is underneath.

2 Whisk the egg whites until they form stiff peaks. Whisk in half each of the caster and muscovado sugar, adding in 25g (1oz) at a time, whisking between each addition until the mixture becomes stiff and satiny looking. Sprinkle the remaining sugar and chopped hazelnuts over the egg whites and use a large metal spoon to fold in lightly.

3 Using the pencil marks as a guide, spread the meringue mixture into rounds on the baking parchment. Sprinkle the remaining chopped nuts over one meringue.

4 Bake for about 1½ hours or until the meringue is well dried out. Leave to cool. When quite cold, peel off the non-stick paper.

5 Meanwhile, prepare the chocolate icing. Melt the chocolate with 150ml (5fl oz) cream (see page 13). Bring to the boil, stirring, then remove from the heat and stir in the ground hazelnuts. Cool, cover and chill until required. Allow the mixture to soften at room temperature for about 1 hour before using.

6 Carefully spread the icing over the meringue round. Top with the remaining whipped cream and finish with the nut-topped meringue round. Chill for 2–3 hours. Serve dusted with icing sugar.

Chocolate and Chestnut Roulade

Hands-on time: 20 minutes · Cooking time: 20–25 minutes, plus cooling
Serves 10: 510 cals, 33g fat (of which 19g saturates), 49g carbohydrate per serving

little vegetable oil
6 medium eggs, separated
200g (7oz) caster sugar, plus extra to dust
2–3 drops vanilla extract
50g (2oz) cocoa powder

For the filling
125g (4oz) plain chocolate, broken into pieces
284ml carton double cream
225g (8oz) unsweetened chestnut purée
200ml tub full-fat crème fraîche
50g (2oz) icing sugar

1 Preheat the oven to 180°C (160°C fan oven) mark 4. Lightly oil a 33 × 20.5cm (13 × 8in) Swiss roll tin, then line it with greaseproof paper.

2 Put the egg yolks into a large bowl. Add the caster sugar and vanilla extract, then whisk until light and pale. Sift in the cocoa powder, then fold in with a large metal spoon. Whisk the egg whites until they form stiff peaks, then fold into the cocoa mixture. Spoon into the prepared tin, spread evenly and bake for 20–25 minutes until just cooked – the top should be springy to the touch.

3 Remove the roulade from the oven and leave to cool in the tin for 10–15 minutes. Put a sheet of baking parchment on to the worksurface and dust with caster sugar. Carefully turn out the roulade on to the parchment, then leave to cool. Peel away the baking parchment.

4 Meanwhile, make the filling. Melt the chocolate (see page 13).

5 In a separate bowl, lightly whip the cream. Beat the chestnut purée into the chocolate until smooth; the mixture will be quite thick. Whisk in the crème fraîche and icing sugar. Beat 1tbsp of the whipped cream into the melted chocolate mixture to loosen it, then use a metal spoon to fold in half the remainder.

6 Spread the filling over the roulade, then spread the remaining cream on top. Roll up the roulade, using the greaseproof paper to help you, and lift on to a serving plate. Dust with caster sugar.

The Ultimate Chocolate Cake

Hands-on time: 15 minutes · Cooking time: 1 hour 20 minutes, plus cooling

Serves 25: 320 cals, 22g fat (of which 10g saturates), 25g carbohydrate per serving

175g (6oz) unsalted butter, softened, plus
    extra to grease
375g (13oz) plain chocolate
175g (6oz) caster sugar
175g (6oz) ground almonds
6 large eggs, separated
75g (3oz) fresh brown breadcrumbs

3tbsp cocoa powder
pinch of salt
125g (4oz) white chocolate, roughly
    chopped
125g (4oz) milk chocolate, roughly chopped
142ml carton double cream

1 Preheat the oven to 180°C (160°C fan oven) mark 4. Grease a 20.5cm (8in) square cake tin and baseline with greaseproof paper.

2 Break 225g (8oz) plain chocolate into a bowl and melt (see page 13). Cool for 10 minutes.

3 Meanwhile, beat the butter and sugar until light and fluffy. Stir in the cooled melted chocolate with the almonds, egg yolks, breadcrumbs and cocoa powder.

4 Whisk the egg whites and salt until they form soft peaks. Fold into the chocolate mixture with the chopped chocolate.

5 Pour the mixture into the prepared tin and bake for about 1 hour 20 minutes, covering loosely with foil if necessary. Cool in the tin for 15 minutes, then turn out on to a wire rack to finish cooling.

6 While the cake is cooling, place the remaining 150g (5oz) plain chocolate and the cream in a bowl and melt (see page 13). Cool for about 30 minutes or until slightly thickened. Pour over the cake to cover and swirl with a palette knife, then leave to cool. Cut up into squares; store in an airtight container for up to five days.

Decadent Chocolate Cake

Hands-on time: 30 minutes · Cooking time: 1½ hours, plus cooling
Serves 12: 690 cals, 50g fat (of which 23g saturates), 50g carbohydrate per serving

300g (11oz) dark chocolate (minimum 70% cocoa solids), broken into pieces
225g (8oz) unsalted butter, softened, plus extra to grease
225g (8oz) golden caster sugar
225g (8oz) ground almonds
8 large eggs, separated
125g (4oz) fresh brown breadcrumbs

4tbsp apricot jam (optional)

For the ganache
175g (6oz) dark chocolate (minimum 70% cocoa solids), broken into pieces
75g (3oz) unsalted butter, softened
4tbsp double cream

1 Preheat the oven to 180°C (160°C fan oven) mark 4. Grease a 23cm (9in) spring-release cake tin and line with greaseproof paper.

2 To make the cake, melt the chocolate (see page 13). Remove from the heat.

3 Put the butter and sugar into a large bowl and beat together until light and creamy. Add the ground almonds, egg yolks and breadcrumbs and beat well until thoroughly mixed. Slowly add the melted chocolate and carefully stir it in, taking care not to over-mix as the chocolate may seize up.

4 Put the egg whites into a clean, grease-free bowl and whisk until they form stiff peaks. Add half the whites to the chocolate mixture and fold in lightly using a large metal spoon, then carefully fold in the remainder.

5 Pour the mixture into the prepared tin and level the surface. Bake for 1 hour 20 minutes or until the cake is firm to the touch and a skewer inserted into the centre comes out clean. Cool in the tin for 5 minutes, then transfer to a rack for 2–3 hours to cool completely.

6 If using, put the jam into a pan and melt over a low heat or heat in a 900W microwave oven on Medium for 50 seconds. Brush jam over the top and sides of the cooled cake.

7 To make the ganache, melt the chocolate, butter and cream in a bowl (see page 13). When melted, stir until smooth. Pour the ganache over the centre of the cake and tip the cake to let it run down the sides evenly, or spread it with a palette knife. Leave to set.

Rich Chocolate Log

Hands-on time: 30 minutes, plus soaking and cooling · Cooking time: 10 minutes

Serves 8: 550 cals, 33g fat (of which 16g saturates), 56g carbohydrate per serving

50g (2oz) seedless raisins
3tbsp Cointreau
125g (4oz) white chocolate
284ml carton double cream

2 x 225g (8oz) chocolate Swiss rolls with
    chocolate butter cream filling, about
    16cm (6½in) long
caramelised hazelnuts (see Cook's Tip) and
    plain chocolate leaves to decorate

1 Put the raisins in a bowl with 2tbsp Cointreau. Cover and leave for about 3 hours.

2 Melt the chocolate (see page 13). Leave to cool for about 10 minutes. Whisk the cream until it just holds its shape and fold in the melted chocolate.

3 Meanwhile, halve each Swiss roll lengthways. Sprinkle over the raisins and Cointreau and sandwich together again.

4 Cut one of the logs in half at an angle. Use one half to extend the other log and place on a serving platter. Place the other half at a right angle to the log to form a branch, securing it with a little of the chocolate mixture.

5 Prick the log all over with a fine skewer and drizzle over the remaining Cointreau.

6 Cover the log with the chocolate mixture. Rough up the surface with a palette knife and decorate with caramelised hazelnuts and chocolate leaves.

COOK'S TIP: To make caramelised hazelnuts, place about 50g (2oz) granulated sugar in a small pan over a low heat. When the sugar has completely dissolved, increase the heat until the liquid turns a pale caramel. Shake the pan gently to distribute the melted sugar evenly, then remove from the heat. Using two forks, dip in the skinned hazelnuts, and stir until coated. Leave to set on foil.

Viennese Chocolate Cake

Hands-on time: 40 minutes · Cooking time: around 1 hour, plus cooling
Serves 12: 470 cals, 34g fat (of which 17g saturates), 38g carbohydrate per serving

little flour to dust
300g (10oz) plain chocolate
150g (5oz) unsalted butter, softened, plus
    extra to grease
125g (4oz) caster sugar
½tsp vanilla extract

5 large eggs, separated
75g (3oz) ground almonds
40g (1½oz) cornflour
6tbsp apricot jam
200ml (7fl oz) double cream
12 truffles

1 Preheat the oven to 180°C (160°C fan oven) mark 4. Grease a 21.5cm (8½in) moule à manqué tin (see page 33) and baseline with greaseproof paper.

2 Melt half the chocolate (see page 13). Take the bowl off the heat and cool slightly. Meanwhile, beat the butter until really soft, preferably using an electric whisk. Gradually beat in the sugar until light and fluffy. Beat in the cooled chocolate and vanilla extract.

3 Whisk the egg whites in a clean, dry mixing bowl. Beat the yolks, one at a time, into the mixture. Gently stir the ground almonds and cornflour into the mixture, which will be quite thick. Add about one-third of the whisked egg whites and stir in vigorously to lighten it. Gently fold in the remaining egg whites. Spoon the mixture into the prepared tin and level the surface.

4 Bake for 55–60 minutes until risen and firm to the touch. The cake may be slightly cracked on top. Leave to cool in the tin for 5 minutes, then invert on to a wire rack. Slide a baking sheet underneath. Peel off the lining paper and leave to cool completely.

5 Heat the jam with 1tbsp water, stirring until evenly blended, then sieve. Brush over the top and sides of the cake to give an even layer. Put to one side to allow to set.

6 Melt the remaining chocolate and the cream (see page 13). Stir occasionally until evenly blended. Cool for 2 minutes.

7 Pour the icing into the centre of the cake and, using a large palette knife, quickly ease it out to the edges of the cake, allowing it to run down the sides. Leave at room temperature until set. Decorate with truffles.

Chocolate and Orange Marble Cake

Hands–on time: 20 minutes · Cooking time: 45 minutes, plus cooling

Serves 8: 620 cals, 40g fat (of which 22g saturates), 62g carbohydrate per serving

175g (6oz) unsalted butter, softened
175g (6oz) golden caster sugar
3 medium eggs
125g (4oz) self-raising flour, sifted
50g (2oz) ground almonds, sifted
1tsp baking powder
finely grated zest of 1 orange

1tbsp brandy
4tbsp cocoa powder, sifted

To finish
200g (7oz) plain chocolate
75g (3oz) unsalted butter

1 Preheat the oven to 190°C (170°C fan oven) mark 5. Line a 900g (2lb) loaf tin with greaseproof paper.

2 To make the cake, cream the butter and sugar in a bowl until pale and light. Beat in the eggs, one at a time.

3 Add the flour, ground almonds and baking powder to the bowl and fold together. Stir in the orange zest and brandy. Put half the mixture into another bowl and mix in the cocoa powder.

4 Spoon a dollop of each mixture into the prepared tin, then repeat with alternate mixtures to create two layers. Shake the tin once, then drag a skewer through the mixture to create a marbled effect. Bake for 45 minutes or until a skewer inserted into the centre comes out clean. Turn out on to a wire rack and cool. Place a tray under the wire rack.

5 To finish, melt the chocolate and butter (see page 13). Pour the chocolate ganache over the cake to completely cover it and leave to set in a cool place for 30 minutes.

White Chocolate Mousse Cake

Hands-on time: 25 minutes · Cooking time: around 1 hour, plus cooling and chilling

Serves 16: 460 cals, 33g fat (of which 18g saturates), 35g carbohydrate per serving

225g (8oz) plain chocolate
9 large eggs
150g (5oz) caster sugar
125g (4oz) unsalted butter, softened, plus
    extra to grease

2tsp powdered gelatine
400g (14oz) white chocolate
300ml (10fl oz) double cream
milk or plain chocolate curls to decorate

1 Preheat the oven to 190°C (170°C fan oven) mark 5. Grease a 20.5cm (8in) spring-release cake tin and baseline with greaseproof paper. Melt the plain chocolate (see page 13) and cool slightly.

2 Meanwhile, using an electric whisk, whisk five egg yolks and the sugar together in a heatproof bowl set over a pan of hot water until thick and creamy. Beat in the butter, a little at a time, until smooth. Off the heat, beat in the melted chocolate. Whisk the five egg whites until they form soft peaks, then gently fold into the chocolate mixture. Pour into the prepared tin, then tap the tin firmly on the worksurface to disperse any bubbles. Bake for 50–55 minutes until risen and firm, covering halfway through cooking with foil. Leave to cool in the tin for 1 hour.

3 To make the mousse layer, sprinkle the gelatine over 2tbsp water in a small heatproof bowl and leave to stand for about 10 minutes. Melt 225g (8oz) white chocolate as in step 1; cool slightly. Beat the remaining four egg yolks into the chocolate, followed by 150ml (5fl oz) cream. Dissolve the gelatine over a pan of gently simmering water. Whisk the remaining four egg whites until they form soft peaks. Stir the gelatine into the chocolate mixture. Stir in a spoonful of egg white to lighten it, then fold in the remainder.

4 Split the cake through the middle. Line the same tin with greaseproof paper and place one round of cake in the base, pressing lightly to fit. Pour over the mousse, then chill for about 30 minutes. Place the remaining cake round on top and chill overnight.

5 To make the icing, place the remaining white chocolate in a bowl with the remaining cream and melt over a pan of gently simmering water until smooth. Cool slightly, beating the mixture until it thickens. Carefully remove the cake from the tin, gently easing away the parchment, and thinly spread over the icing, then chill to set. Decorate with milk or plain chocolate curls.

Cherry Chocolate Pudding

Hands-on time: 15 minutes · Cooking time: 55 minutes, plus cooling

Serves 6: 570 cals, 31g fat (of which 18g saturates), 71g carbohydrate per serving

425g can pitted black cherries in syrup, drained and syrup reserved, cherries halved

125g (4oz) golden caster sugar

125g (4oz) unsalted butter, plus extra to grease

250g (9oz) plain chocolate, roughly chopped

2 medium eggs

1tsp vanilla extract

75g (3oz) self-raising flour, sifted

1 Preheat the oven to 190°C (170°C fan oven) mark 5. Grease an 18cm (7in) square cake tin and baseline with greaseproof paper.

2 Put the reserved cherry syrup in a small pan with 25g (1oz) sugar. Bring to the boil and simmer until reduced by half. Cool.

3 Put the butter in a small heatproof bowl with 75g (3oz) chocolate and melt (see page 13). Remove from the heat and cool. Put the eggs in a bowl with the remaining sugar and the vanilla extract and beat together until the mixture is thick and pale. Fold in the cooled chocolate mixture, along with the flour and remaining chocolate.

4 Arrange the cherries in the bottom of the prepared tin and pour over the chocolate mixture. Bake for 30 minutes, then cover with foil and bake for a further 15 minutes. Leave to cool for 5 minutes in the tin, then turn out by covering with a large plate or board and carefully inverting it. Pour over the reserved cherry syrup while the cake is still warm. Serve with ready-made fresh vanilla custard.

Chocolate and Cherry Cups

Hands-on time: 15 minutes · Cooking time: none

Serves 4: 590 cals, 43g fat (of which 26g saturates), 43g carbohydrate per serving

425g can pitted black cherries in syrup
2tbsp brandy
250g (9oz) mascarpone cheese
1tbsp caster sugar
2 amaretti biscuits

4tbsp single cream
4 ready-made chocolate cups
cocoa powder for dusting
chocolate curls to decorate
single cream to serve

1 Drain the cherries and put in a bowl. Add 1tbsp brandy, cover and put to one side. Put the mascarpone in a bowl with the sugar and remaining brandy, then gently beat. Crumble the amaretti biscuits and fold, with the cream, into the mascarpone.

2 Divide the cherries among the chocolate cups, then spoon in the mascarpone mixture. Chill.

3 Put the cups on individual serving plates, dust with cocoa powder, decorate with plain or milk chocolate curls and serve with single cream.

CHEESECAKE DELIGHTS

B iscuit bases and cream cheese – you can't go wrong with a solid chunk of cheesecake. The Jewelled Cheesecake is studded with glacé fruits, candied peel and pistachio nuts and the Classic Baked Lemon Cheesecake combines a buttery biscuit base with a dense topping of curd cheese, eggs and dried fruit, flavoured with zesty lemon.

Raspberry Cheesecake

Ginger and Lemon Cheesecake

Crumbly Apple and Cheese Cake

Blueberry Cheesecake

Classic Baked Lemon Cheesecake

Lemon Cheesecake

Warm Ginger Ricotta Cake

Chocolate and Orange Cheesecake

Toffee Cheesecake

Jewelled Cheesecake

Raspberry Cheesecake

Hands-on time: 25 minutes, plus chilling · Cooking time: 5 minutes

Serves 10–12: 270–230 cals, 15–13g fat (of which 8–7g saturates), 28g–23g carbohydrate per serving

For the base
25g (1oz) blanched almonds
225g (8oz) almond butter biscuits, crushed
100g (3½oz) melted butter
few drops almond extract

For the filling
450g (1lb) raspberries
300ml (10fl oz) Greek yogurt
150g (5oz) low-fat soft cheese
1tbsp powdered gelatine
2 medium egg whites
50g (2oz) icing sugar

1 Grease a 22cm (8½in) round spring-release cake tin.

2 To make the base, lightly toast the almonds, then finely chop. Mix the almonds with the crushed biscuits and melted butter. Add the almond extract. Spoon into the tin, then press down with the back of a spoon. Chill.

3 To make the filling, purée 225g (8oz) raspberries in a blender, then press through a sieve. Reserve three-quarters of the purée; return the rest to the blender, add the yogurt and cheese, then whiz until well blended. Transfer to a bowl.

4 Sprinkle the gelatine over 2tbsp water in a small heatproof bowl and leave to soak for 2–3 minutes. Place the bowl over a pan of simmering water until the gelatine has dissolved.

5 Whisk the egg whites with the icing sugar until very thick and shiny. Fold into the cheese mixture.

6 Arrange half the remaining berries over the biscuit base. Pour the cheese mixture over the berries. Spoon in the reserved purée and swirl with a knife to make a marbled pattern. Sprinkle with the remaining raspberries and chill for 3–4 hours or until set.

Ginger and Lemon Cheesecake

Hands-on time: 20 minutes · Cooking time: 55 minutes, plus cooling
Serves 6: 530 cals, 35g fat (of which 20g saturates) 49g carbohydrate per serving

175g (6oz) digestive biscuits
25g (1oz) unsalted butter, melted
3 balls of stem ginger – about 50g (2oz)
   total weight
2 x 200g (7oz) packs full-fat soft cheese

zest of 1 large or 2 small lemons and
   4tbsp lemon juice
125g (4oz) caster sugar
4tbsp crème fraîche
1 medium egg
icing sugar for dusting

1 Preheat the oven to 180°C (160°C fan oven) mark 4. Line the base of an 18cm (7in) spring-release tin with greaseproof paper.

2 Place the biscuits, butter and ginger in a food processor and blend until crumbed, then press into the base of the tin. Bake for 15 minutes or until just beginning to change colour.

3 Place all the remaining ingredients except the icing sugar into a food processor and blend until smooth. Spoon the cheese mixture on to the warm biscuit base and bake for 35–40 minutes or until just set. Cool in the tin for 30 minutes.

4 Loosen the edges of the cheesecake, then remove the sides of the tin. Leave on the tin base and serve warm, generously dusted with icing sugar. Any leftover cheesecake can be kept in the fridge and served chilled.

Crumbly Apple and Cheese Cake

Hands-on time: 20 minutes, plus cooling · Cooking time: 50-60 minutes

Serves 10: 350 cals, 20g fat (of which 7g saturates), 34g carbohydrate per slice

90ml (3fl oz) sunflower oil, plus extra to
    grease
550g (1¼lb) dessert apples, peeled, cored
    and thinly sliced
50g (2oz) Brazil nuts, roughly chopped
175g (6oz) self-raising flour
1tsp baking powder

75g (3oz) light muscovado sugar
50g (2oz) raisins
50g (2oz) sultanas
2 medium eggs
225g (8oz) Caerphilly or Wensleydale cheese
icing sugar for dusting

1 Preheat the oven to 180°C (160°C fan oven) mark 4. Grease a 5cm (2in) deep, 23cm (9in) round loose-base flan tin and baseline with greaseproof paper.

2 Sift the flour and baking powder into a bowl. Stir in the sugar, raisins, sultanas, nuts and apples, and mix until combined. Beat the eggs with the oil and add to the dry ingredients. Stir until evenly incorporated.

3 Spoon half the mixture into the prepared tin and level the surface. Crumble the cheese over the surface, then spoon on the remaining cake mix. Spread it to the edges of the tin, but do not smooth.

4 Bake for 50–60 minutes or until golden and just firm. Leave to cool in the tin for 10 minutes, then transfer to a wire rack. Serve warm, dusted with icing sugar.

Blueberry Cheesecake

Hands-on time: 15 minutes · Cooking time: around 45 minutes, plus chilling

Serves 8: 410 cals, 29g fat (of which 16g saturates), 33g carbohydrate per serving

butter, to grease
200g (7oz) flan case
300g pack cream cheese
1tsp vanilla extract
100g (3½oz) golden caster sugar

142ml carton soured cream
2 medium eggs
2tbsp cornflour
150g (5oz) blueberries
2tbsp redcurrant jelly

1 Preheat the oven to 180°C (160°C fan oven) mark 4. Use the base of a 20.5cm (8in) spring-release cake tin as a guide to cut out a circle from the flan case, discarding (or eating!) the edges. Grease the tin, then put the flan base into it. Press down with your fingers.

2 Put the cream cheese, vanilla extract, sugar, soured cream, eggs and cornflour into a processor and whiz until evenly combined.

3 Pour the mixture over the flan base and shake gently to level. Bake for 45 minutes until just set and pale golden. Turn off the oven and leave the cheesecake inside with the door ajar for about 30 minutes. Cool and chill.

4 To serve, put the blueberries into a pan with the redcurrant jelly and heat through until the jelly has melted and the blueberries have softened slightly, or heat in a 900W microwave oven on High for 1 minute. Spoon on top of the cheesecake. Cool and chill for 15 minutes before serving.

Classic Baked Lemon Cheesecake

Hands-on time: 30 minutes, plus chilling · Cooking time: 55 minutes
Serves 12: 360 cals, 21g fat (of which 12g saturates), 36g carbohydrate per serving

For the base
250g packet digestive biscuits
125g (4oz) unsalted butter, plus extra to
  grease

For the filling
1 large unwaxed lemon

2 × 250g tubs curd cheese
142ml carton soured cream
2 medium eggs
175g (6oz) golden caster sugar
1½tsp vanilla extract
1tbsp cornflour
50g (2oz) sultanas

1 Grease a 20.5cm (8in) spring-release cake tin. For the base, put the biscuits in a food processor and whiz until fine. Melt the butter, add to the biscuits and mix in the processor until well combined. Tip the mixture into the prepared tin. Using the back of a spoon, press evenly into the base. Chill for 1 hour until firm.

2 Preheat the oven to 180°C (160°C fan oven) mark 4. Grate the zest from the lemon and put to one side. Halve the lemon, cut three thin slices from one half and put to one side. Squeeze the juice from the lemon into a small bowl or cup.

3 To make the filling, put the lemon zest, lemon juice, curd cheese, soured cream, eggs, sugar, vanilla extract and cornflour into a large bowl. Using an electric mixer, whisk together until thick and smooth, then fold in the sultanas.

4 Pour the mixture on to the biscuit base and shake gently to level. Bake for 30 minutes. Put the lemon slices, overlapping, on top. Bake for another 20–25 minutes until just set and golden brown. Turn off the oven, leaving the cheesecake inside and the door ajar. When the cheesecake is cool, chill for at least 2 hours or overnight.

5 Remove the cheesecake from the fridge half an hour before serving. Run a knife around the edge and sit the tin on an upturned bowl. Release the side of the tin and remove. Slide a palette knife or fish slice under the base and carefully move the cheesecake on to a serving plate.

Lemon Cheesecake

Hands-on time: 25 minutes, plus chilling · Cooking time: 5 minutes

Serves 6: 330 cals, 19g fat (of which 10g saturates), 31g carbohydrate per serving

For the base
175g (6oz) digestive biscuits, crushed
75g (3oz) unsalted butter, melted, plus
   extra to grease

For the filling
zest and juice of 2 lemons

1tbsp powdered gelatine
225g (8oz) low-fat soft cheese
150ml (5fl oz) natural yogurt
4tbsp clear honey
2 medium egg whites
blanched shredded lemon zest to decorate

1 Grease a 20.5cm (8in) spring-release cake tin. To make the base, stir the crushed biscuits into the melted butter and mix well. Press the mixture into the base of the prepared tin. Chill until firm while making the filling.

2 To make the filling, make up the juice from the lemons to 150ml (5fl oz) with water. Sprinkle the gelatine over the lemon juice and water in a heatproof bowl and leave to soak for 2–3 minutes. Place the bowl over a pan of simmering water until the gelatine dissolves. Leave to cool slightly.

3 Whisk the cheese, yogurt and honey together in a bowl. Stir in the lemon zest and dissolved gelatine until thoroughly mixed. Whisk the egg whites until they form soft peaks. Fold into the cheesecake mixture. Spoon onto the biscuit base and level the surface. Chill for at least 4 hours until set.

4 Remove the cheesecake from the tin and decorate with the blanched lemon shreds to serve.

Warm Ginger Ricotta Cake

Hands-on time: 25 minutes · Cooking time: 1¼ hours, plus cooling

Serves 6–8: 620–460 cals, 41–30g fat (of which 22–17g saturates), 54–41g carbohydrate per serving

225g (8oz) digestive biscuits
75g (3oz) unsalted butter, melted, plus extra
   to grease
1 ball of stem ginger in syrup, plus 1tbsp
   syrup
200g tub full-fat soft cheese

225g (8oz) ricotta cheese
4tbsp double cream
3 medium eggs, separated
1tbsp cornflour
125g (4oz) icing sugar

1 Preheat the oven to 200°C (180°C fan oven) mark 6. Crush the biscuits in a blender or processor to a fine powder, then pour on the melted butter. Whiz the mixture for a further minute.

2 Grease a 20.5cm (8in) spring-release tin and completely cover with just over half the crumb mixture. Put to one side.

3 Finely chop the stem ginger. Beat or whiz together the cheeses, cream, egg yolks, cornflour, ginger and syrup. The mixture should be creamy and the ginger roughly chopped through it. Transfer to a large bowl.

4 Whisk the egg whites until they form soft peaks. Gradually whisk in the icing sugar, keeping the meringue very stiff and shiny. Fold into the ginger mixture and spoon on to the biscuit base. Sprinkle over the remaining biscuit crumbs.

5 Bake for 30 minutes. Reduce the oven temperature to 180°C (160°C fan oven) mark 4, cover the cake loosely with foil and bake for a further 45 minutes. The cake should feel just set in the centre. Remove and cool for 15 minutes on a wire rack (it will sink a bit). Serve warm.

COOK'S TIP: Serve the cake with Ginger and Whisky Sauce (see page 17). The cake may also be served with sliced oranges soaked in ginger syrup and Cointreau.

Chocolate and Orange Cheesecake

Hands-on time: 35 minutes · Cooking time: 1 hour 10 minutes, plus cooling

Serves 6–8: 640–480 cals, 47g–35g fat (of which 28g–21g saturates), 41g–31g carbohydrate per serving

3 medium eggs
125g (4oz) caster sugar
3 × 200g tubs full-fat soft cheese
6tbsp crème fraîche or thick Greek yogurt
125g (4oz) plain chocolate

zest of 2 large oranges
orange segments and chocolate curls to
  decorate
icing sugar to dust

1 Preheat the oven to 180°C (160°C fan oven) mark 4. Grease a 23cm (9in) spring-release cake tin and baseline with non-stick baking parchment.

2 Separate the eggs. Beat the egg yolks with 50g (2oz) caster sugar until pale in colour and thick. Add the soft cheese and crème fraîche or Greek yogurt and beat until smooth.

3 Melt the chocolate (see page 13). Add one-third of the cheese mixture to the chocolate, mix until smooth and put to one side. Add the orange zest to the remaining cheese mixture.

4 Whisk the egg whites until they form stiff peaks and then gradually whisk in the remaining sugar until the mixture is stiff and shiny.

5 Fold one-third of the egg whites into the chocolate mixture, spoon into the prepared tin and smooth the top. Fold the remaining egg whites into the orange mixture, spoon on top of the chocolate mixture and level the top.

6 Bake for 55–60 minutes or until the centre is just firm to the touch. Turn off the oven and allow the cheesecake to cool in the oven.

7 Decorate with orange segments, chocolate curls and a dusting of icing sugar.

Toffee Cheesecake

Hands-on time: 15 minutes, plus chilling · Cooking time: 55-60 minutes
Serves 10: 460 cals, 32g fat (of which 17g saturates), 34g carbohydrate per serving

For the crust
300g packet digestive biscuits, broken
125g (4oz) unsalted butter, melted

For the filling
450g (1lb) curd cheese

142ml carton double cream
juice of ½ lemon
3 medium eggs, beaten
50g (2oz) golden caster sugar
6tbsp Banoffee Toffee Sauce, plus extra to
   drizzle

1 Preheat the oven to 200°C (180°C fan oven) mark 6.

2 To make the crust, put the biscuits into a food processor and whiz until fine. Add the butter and pulse briefly to combine. Press the mixture evenly into the base and up the sides of a 20.5cm (8in) spring-release cake tin. Chill in the fridge.

3 To make the filling, put the curd cheese and cream in a food processor and whiz until smooth. Add the lemon juice, eggs, sugar and toffee sauce, then whiz again until smooth. Pour on to the chilled biscuit case and bake for 10 minutes. Reduce the oven temperature to 180°C (160°C fan oven) mark 4, then bake for 45 minutes or until set and golden brown.

4 Turn off the oven, leave the door ajar and let the cheesecake cool. When completely cool, chill to firm up the crust.

5 Remove the cheesecake from the tin by running a knife around the edge. Open the tin carefully, then use a palette knife to ease the cheesecake out. Cut into wedges, put on a serving plate, then drizzle with toffee sauce straight from the bottle.

COOK'S TIP: To slice the cheesecake easily, use a sharp knife dipped into a jug of boiling water and wiped dry.

Jewelled Cheesecake

Hands-on time: 20 minutes · Cooking time: 50–55 minutes, plus cooling

Serves 8: 560 cals, 42g fat (of which 24g saturates), 39g carbohydrate per serving

200g (7oz) sponge flan case
2tbsp orange-flavour liqueur, such as
  Cointreau or Grand Marnier (optional)
500g (1lb 2oz) cream cheese
125g (4oz) golden caster sugar
3 medium eggs

zest of ½ orange
40g (1½oz) chopped mixed peel
50g (2oz) natural colour glacé cherries,
  thinly sliced
25g (1oz) pistachio nuts, chopped
raspberry coulis to serve

1 Preheat the oven to 180°C (160°C fan oven) mark 4. Grease a 23cm (9in) spring-release cake tin and line with greaseproof paper. Cut off the raised edge of the sponge flan case so that it fits snugly inside the tin. You can reserve the edges for a trifle or just eat them – the cook's perk! If using, drizzle the liqueur over the sponge base.

2 Put the cream cheese in a large bowl. Add the caster sugar and beat together, then mix in the eggs. Add the orange zest, mixed peel, glacé cherries and pistachio nuts and mix well. Spoon the mixture on to the sponge base and level the top. Bake for 50–55 minutes until slightly risen and firm to the touch. Leave to cool in the tin.

3 Carefully remove the cheesecake from the tin. Put it on a plate, cut into slices and drizzle with a little raspberry coulis.

TEATIME TREATS

Muffins, cakes, flapjacks and sweet loaves are all delicious treats at teatime, easy to make and just the thing for when friends pop round or the kids get home from school. The Almond and Polenta Cake is a simple, yet sophisticated accompaniment to a cup of coffee. The Blueberry Muffins are juicy and tasty – Americans would serve these for breakfast but they're great at any time of the day!

Basic Muffin Mixture

Bran and Apple Muffins

Almond and Polenta Cake

Pineapple and Coconut Loaf

Lamingtons

Blueberry Muffins

Lemon Seed Loaf

Lime Drizzle Loaf

Blackberry and Cinnamon Yogurt Loaf

Spiced Carrot Muffins

Vanilla Crumble Bars

Hazelnut and Chocolate Flapjacks

Chocolate Pecan Bars

Teatime Cherry Cake

Cherry and Almond Muffins

Basic Muffin Mixture

Hands-on time: 10 minutes · Cooking time: 30–35 minutes

Serves 6: 240 cals, 8g fat (of which 5g saturates), 39g carbohydrate per serving

12 brown sugar cubes
150g (5oz) plain flour
1½tsp baking powder
¼tsp salt
1 medium egg, beaten

40g (1½oz) golden caster sugar
50g (2oz) unsalted butter, melted
½tsp vanilla extract
100ml (3½fl oz) milk

1 Preheat the oven to 200°C (180°C fan oven) mark 6. Line a muffin tin with 6 muffin cases.

2 Roughly crush the sugar cubes and put to one side. Sift together the flour, baking powder and salt.

3 In a large bowl, combine the beaten egg, caster sugar, melted butter, vanilla extract and milk.

4 Fold in the sifted flour and spoon the mixture into muffin cases. Sprinkle with the brown sugar. Bake for 30–35 minutes. Cool on a wire rack.

VARIATIONS

Apple and Cinnamon

240 cals, 8g fat (of which 5g saturates), 41g carbohydrate per serving
Fold 5tbsp ready-made chunky apple sauce and 1tsp ground cinnamon into the basic mixture with the flour and complete as above.

Maple Syrup and Pecan

320 cals, 14g fat (of which 5g saturates), 46g carbohydrate per serving
Lightly toast 50g (2oz) pecan nuts and roughly chop. Fold half the nuts and 3tbsp maple syrup into the basic mixture. Mix the remaining nuts with the crushed sugar and sprinkle over the muffins before baking. Drizzle with maple syrup to serve.

Bran and Apple Muffins

Hands–on time: 20 minutes · Cooking time: 30 minutes

Serves 10: 150 cals, 1g fat (of which trace saturates), 33g carbohydrate per serving

250ml (8fl oz) semi-skimmed milk
2tbsp orange juice
50g (2oz) All Bran
150g (5oz) prune purée
100g (3½oz) light muscovado sugar
2 medium egg whites

1tbsp golden syrup
150g (5oz) plain flour
1tsp baking powder
1tsp ground cinnamon
1 eating apple, peeled and grated
demerara sugar to sprinkle

1 Preheat the oven to 190°C (170°C fan oven) mark 5. Line a muffin tin with 10 muffin cases.

2 In a bowl, mix the milk and orange juice with the All Bran. Put to one side for 10 minutes.

3 In a large bowl, cream together the prune purée and muscovado sugar. Add the egg whites, golden syrup and the milk mixture.

4 Sift the flour, baking powder and cinnamon together and add to the mixture along with the grated apple. Mix well.

5 Spoon the mixture into the muffin cases and bake for 30 minutes or until well risen and golden brown. Sprinkle with demerara sugar just before serving.

Almond and Polenta Cake

Hands-on time: 5 minutes · Cooking time: 40 minutes, plus cooling

Serves 8: 590 cals, 40g fat (of which 16g saturates), 52g carbohydrate per slice

150g (5oz) each caster sugar and ground almonds
150g (5oz) 'quick-cook' polenta
(see Cook's Tip)

150g (5oz) unsalted butter, softened, plus extra to grease

1 Preheat the oven to 190°C (170°C fan oven) mark 5. Grease an 18cm (7in) loose-base fluted flan tin.

2 Mix all the dry ingredients together in a bowl and stir in the softened butter until it is well blended. Press this mixture into the prepared tin, making sure that it is evenly spread.

3 Bake for 40 minutes or until golden brown and firm to the touch. Allow to cool in the tin, then turn out to cool completely on a wire rack.

4 Serve, sliced, with a glass of chilled dessert wine or a cup of coffee.

COOK'S TIP: Yellow polenta is coarsely ground maize that is usually cooked with water to a soft 'porridge' or a firm 'cake' and served as an accompaniment to savoury dishes. It can also be used to give a crumbly texture to bakes. 'Quick-cook' polenta, which is perfect for this recipe, is a pre-cooked, fine type of polenta, available from delicatessens and major supermarkets.

Pineapple and Coconut Loaf

Hands-on time: 20 minutes · Cooking time: 50 minutes, plus cooling

Serves 10: 240 cals, 13g fat (of which 8g saturates), 28g carbohydrate per slice

125g (4oz) unsalted butter, plus extra to
    grease
432g can pineapple in natural juice
150g (5oz) wholemeal flour, sifted
125g (4oz) dark muscovado sugar
2 medium eggs

2tsp baking powder
¼tsp mixed spice
50g (2oz) desiccated coconut
extra desiccated coconut and icing sugar
    to decorate

1 Preheat the oven to 180°C (160°C fan oven) mark 4. Grease a 450g (1lb) loaf tin and baseline with greaseproof paper.

2 Drain the pineapple well and roughly chop. Put the flour and muscovado sugar in a food processor and whiz for 1–2 minutes until well mixed. Add the remaining ingredients and mix until smooth.

3 Turn the mixture into the prepared tin, level the surface and brush lightly with 2tbsp cold water. Bake for 50 minutes or until a skewer inserted into the centre comes out clean (if necessary, cover lightly with foil after 40 minutes).

4 Allow the cake to cool in the tin for 10 minutes, then transfer to a wire rack to cool completely. Decorate with a little desiccated coconut and icing sugar.

Lamingtons

Hands-on time: 40 minutes, plus cooling and setting · Cooking time: 30 minutes

Serves 16: 280 cals, 18g fat (of which 12g saturates), 31g carbohydrate per slice

125g (4oz) unsalted butter, softened, plus
  extra to grease
125g (4oz) golden caster sugar
2 medium eggs
125g (4oz) self-raising flour, sifted
1tsp baking powder
2tsp vanilla extract

For the icing
200g (7oz) icing sugar
50g (2oz) cocoa powder
25g (1oz) unsalted butter
5 tbsp milk
200g (7oz) desiccated coconut

1 Preheat the oven to 180°C (160°C fan oven) mark 4. Grease a 15cm (6in) square cake tin and line with greaseproof paper.

2 To make the sponge, put the butter, sugar, eggs, flour, baking powder and vanilla extract in a bowl and beat with an electric whisk until creamy. Turn the mixture into the prepared tin and level. Bake for about 30 minutes until just firm to the touch and a skewer inserted into the centre comes out clean. Transfer to a wire rack to cool. Wrap and store, preferably overnight, so the cake is easier to slice.

3 To make the icing, sift the icing sugar and cocoa powder into a bowl. Cut the butter into pieces and heat in a small saucepan with the milk until the butter has just melted. Pour the liquid over the icing sugar and stir until smooth, adding 2–3tbsp water so the icing thickly coats the back of a spoon.

4 Trim the side crusts from the cake and cut into 16 small squares. Position a sheet of greaseproof paper under a wire rack to catch the drips. Scatter the coconut on to a large plate.

5 Pierce a piece of cake through the top crust and dip into the icing until coated, turning the cake gently. Transfer to the wire rack. Once you've coated half the pieces, roll them in the coconut and transfer to a plate. Repeat with the remainder and leave to set for a couple of hours before serving.

COOK'S TIP: If at the end of coating the sponge the chocolate mixture has thickened, thin down with a drop of water and carefully stir in.

Blueberry Muffins

Hands-on time: 10 minutes · Cooking time: 20–25 minutes

Serves 12: 210 cals, 2g fat (of which 0g saturates), 47g carbohydrate per serving

2 medium eggs
250ml (8fl oz) semi-skimmed milk
250g (9oz) golden granulated sugar
2tsp vanilla extract

350g (12oz) plain flour
4tsp baking powder
250g (9oz) blueberries, frozen
finely grated zest of 2 lemons

1 Preheat the oven to 200°C (180°C fan oven) mark 6. Line a muffin tin with 12 muffin cases and put to one side.

2 Put the eggs, milk, sugar and vanilla extract in a bowl and mix well.

3 In another bowl, sift the flour and baking powder together, then add the blueberries and lemon zest. Toss together, then make a well in the centre.

4 Pour the wet ingredients into the dry ingredients and mix in gently, as overbeating will make the muffins tough.

5 Divide the mixture among the muffin cases and bake for 20–25 minutes. These are best enjoyed on the day.

Lemon Seed Loaf

Hands-on time: 20 minutes · Cooking time: 1 hour, plus cooling
Serves 12: 210 cals, 6g fat (of which 3g saturates), 40g carbohydrate per slice

3 lemons
50g (2oz) unsalted butter, plus extra
    to grease
250g (9oz) caster sugar
250g (9oz) self-raising flour, sifted

1tsp baking powder
1 medium egg
100ml (3½fl oz) semi-skimmed milk
2tbsp plain yogurt
2tbsp poppy seeds

1 Preheat the oven to 180°C (160°C fan oven) mark 4. Lightly grease a 900g (2lb) loaf tin and baseline with greaseproof paper.

2 Remove the zest from one of the lemons. Whiz the butter in a food processor until soft. Add the lemon zest, 200g (7oz) sugar, the flour, baking powder, egg, milk, yogurt and poppy seeds. Whiz until smooth.

3 Turn the mixture into the prepared tin and level the top. Bake for 55–60 minutes until cooked through (cover lightly with foil after 40 minutes, if necessary). Cool in the tin for 10 minutes.

4 For the syrup, squeeze the juice from the lemon with the zest removed, plus one more lemon. Thinly slice the third lemon. Place together in a pan with the remaining sugar and 150ml (5fl oz) water. Bring to the boil, then bubble for 4–5 minutes until syrupy. Remove from the heat.

5 Loosen the sides of the cake with a knife and turn out. Using a cocktail stick, pierce the cake in several places. Spoon the syrup and lemon slices over. Leave to set.

Lime Drizzle Loaf

Hands-on time: 15 minutes · Cooking time: 45–55 minutes, plus cooling

Serves 12: 300 cals, 16g fat (of which 9g saturates), 40g carbohydrate per square

175g (6oz) self-raising flour, sifted with a
  pinch of salt
175g (6oz) unsalted butter, plus extra to
  grease
175g (6oz) golden caster sugar
3 medium eggs, beaten
50g (2oz) sweetened and tenderised
  coconut

zest and juice of 2 limes
1tsp baking powder

For the icing
1 lime
125g (4oz) golden icing sugar, sifted
1tbsp sweetened and tenderised coconut to
  decorate

1 Preheat the oven to 180°C (160°C fan oven) mark 4. Baseline a 900g (2lb) loaf tin with greaseproof paper.

2 Put the flour, butter, caster sugar, eggs, coconut, lime zest and juice and baking powder in the bowl of a freestanding mixer. Mix together slowly, then gradually increase the speed and mix for 2 minutes.

3 Pour the mixture (it'll be quite runny) into the prepared tin and bake for 45–55 minutes until golden, well risen and cooked through – a skewer inserted into the centre should come out clean. Leave to cool for 10 minutes, then lift out the cake, keeping it in the liner.

4 To make the icing, finely grate the zest from the lime and cut away the white pith. Chop the lime flesh, then put in a mini processor with the zest and whiz for 1–2 minutes until finely chopped. Add the icing sugar and blend until smooth. Pour over the cake, then sprinkle the coconut on top to decorate.

Blackberry and Cinnamon Yogurt Loaf

Hands-on time: 15 minutes · Cooking time: 55 minutes

Serves 8: 330 cals, 18g fat (of which 3g saturates), 38g carbohydrate per serving

125ml (4fl oz) sunflower oil, plus extra to
    grease
175g (6oz) plain flour
1½tsp baking powder
1½tsp ground cinnamon
200g (7oz) frozen blackberries

125g (4oz) golden caster sugar
zest and juice of 1 lemon
125ml (4fl oz) Greek yogurt
3 medium eggs, beaten
golden icing sugar to dust

1 Preheat the oven to 190°C (170°C fan oven) mark 5. Grease a 900g (2lb) loaf tin and baseline with greaseproof paper.

2 Sift the flour, baking powder and cinnamon into a bowl, add the frozen berries and toss to coat. Make a well in the centre.

3 In another bowl, whisk together the caster sugar, oil, lemon zest and juice, yogurt and eggs. Pour into the well in the flour mixture and stir.

4 Spoon the mixture into the prepared tin, level the surface and bake for 55 minutes (cover with foil if the top is browning too quickly) or until a skewer inserted into the centre comes out clean. Leave in the tin to cool. When cool, dust with icing sugar.

Spiced Carrot Muffins

Hands-on time: 30 minutes · Cooking time: 20–25 minutes, plus cooling

Serves 12: 340 cals, 22g fat (of which 11g saturates), 33g carbohydrate per serving

125g (4oz) unsalted butter, softened
125g (4oz) light muscovado sugar
3 balls of stem ginger, drained and chopped
150g (5oz) self-raising flour, sifted
1½tsp baking powder
1tbsp ground mixed spice
25g (1oz) ground almonds
3 medium eggs, lightly beaten
finely grated zest of ½ orange
150g (5oz) carrots, grated

50g (2oz) pecan nuts, chopped
50g (2oz) sultanas
3tbsp white rum or orange liqueur
  (optional)

For the icing
200g (7oz) full-fat cream cheese
75g (3oz) icing sugar
1tsp lemon juice
12 sugar roses to decorate (optional)

1 Preheat the oven to 180°C (160°C fan oven) mark 4. Line two muffin trays each with 12 paper muffin cases.

2 Beat together the butter, muscovado sugar and stem ginger until pale and creamy.

3 Add the flour, baking powder, spice, ground almonds, eggs and orange zest and beat well until combined.

4 Stir in the grated carrot, pecan nuts and sultanas. Divide the mixture among the muffin cases and bake for about 20–25 minutes until risen and just firm. A skewer inserted into the centre should come out clean. Transfer to a wire rack and leave to cool.

5 To make the icing, beat the cream cheese in a bowl until softened. Beat in the icing sugar and lemon juice to give a smooth icing that just holds its shape.

6 Drizzle each cake with a little liqueur, if using. Use a small palette knife to spread a little icing over each cake. Decorate each cake with a sugar rose, if using.

Vanilla Crumble Bars

Hands-on time: 15 minutes · Cooking time: 50-60 minutes

Serves 25: 170 cals, 9g fat (of which 5g saturates), 20g carbohydrate per serving

250g (9oz) unsalted butter, softened, plus
    extra to grease
250g (9oz) caster sugar
125g (4oz) plain flour, sifted

175g (6oz) self-raising flour
zest of 1 lemon
3 large eggs
1½tsp vanilla extract

1 Preheat the oven to 180°C (160°C fan oven) mark 4. Grease a 4cm (1½in) deep, 26 × 16cm (10¼ × 6½in) tin and line with greaseproof paper.

2 Put 75g (3oz) of the butter and 75g (3oz) of the sugar in a food processor and blend until smooth. Add the plain flour and blend for 8–10 seconds to very rough breadcrumbs, then put to one side.

3 Put the remaining butter and sugar, the self-raising flour, lemon zest, eggs and vanilla extract in the food processor and whiz for about 15 seconds or until smooth. Pour the mixture into the prepared tin, sprinkle the crumble topping over the surface of the mixture and press down to cover.

4 Bake for 50–60 minutes, covering loosely with foil if necessary. Remove from the oven and cool for 5 minutes, then turn out on to a wire rack. Cut up and store in an airtight container for up to three days.

VARIATION:

Cherry and Coconut Crumble Bars

200 cals, 11g fat (of which 6g saturates), 26g carbohydrate per bar
Make the base as above, adding 50g (2oz) desiccated coconut at the end of step 2. Rinse and dry 225g (8oz) glacé cherries and quarter; fold in the cherries at the end of stage 3. Cook as above.

Hazelnut and Chocolate Flapjacks

Hands-on time: 10 minutes · Cooking time: 30 minutes, plus cooling
Serves 12: 220 cals, 13g fat (of which 6g saturates), 24g carbohydrate per serving

125g (4oz) unsalted butter, plus extra to
   grease
50g (2oz) hazelnuts
125g (4oz) light muscovado sugar

1tbsp golden syrup
175g (6oz) jumbo or porridge oats
50g (2oz) plain chocolate, roughly chopped

1 Preheat the oven to 180°C (160°C fan oven) mark 4. Lightly grease a 28 × 18cm (11 × 7in) shallow oblong baking tin. Roughly chop the hazelnuts.

2 Melt together the butter, sugar and syrup. Stir in the hazelnuts and oats. Allow to cool slightly, then stir in the chocolate.

3 Spoon the mixture into the prepared tin and bake for about 30 minutes or until golden and firm.

4 Cool in the tin for a few minutes, then cut into squares. Turn out on to a wire rack and leave to cool completely.

Chocolate Pecan Bars

Hands-on time: 15 minutes · Cooking time: 1¼ hours, plus cooling
Serves 25: 200 cals, 13g fat (of which 6g saturates), 20g carbohydrate per serving

125g (4oz) plain flour, sifted
25g (1oz) icing sugar
190g (6½oz) unsalted butter, plus extra to
    grease
1 large egg yolk and 2 large eggs
125g (4oz) self-raising flour
1tsp baking powder

125g (4oz) caster sugar
3–4 drops vanilla extract
150g (5oz) milk chocolate chips
75g (3oz) pecan nuts, chopped
6tbsp chocolate and hazelnut spread,
    such as Nutella

1 Preheat the oven to 200°C (180°C fan oven) mark 6. Grease a 4cm (1½in) deep, 26 × 16cm (10¼ × 6½in) cake tin and baseline with greaseproof paper. Put the plain flour and icing sugar in a food processor with 65g (2½oz) roughly chopped butter and whiz until crumb-like in texture. Add the egg yolk and whiz for 10–15 seconds or until the mixture begins to come together. Turn into the tin and press into a thin layer. Bake for 15 minutes or until golden.

2 Meanwhile, place the self-raising flour, baking powder, caster sugar, vanilla extract and the remaining eggs in the food processor with 125g (4oz) softened butter and blend for 15 seconds or until smooth. Remove the blade and fold in the chocolate chips and pecan nuts. Set aside.

3 Spread the chocolate and hazelnut spread over the cooked base and top with the cake mixture. Reduce the oven temperature to 180°C (160°C fan oven) mark 4 and bake for 45–50 minutes until golden – cover loosely with foil if necessary. Cool for about 10 minutes, then turn out on to a wire rack to cool completely. Cut up and store in an airtight container for up to two days.

VARIATION

Date and Banana Bars

150 cals, 8g fat (of which 4g saturates), 20g carbohydrate per bar
Make as above, omitting the chocolate chips, pecan nuts and chocolate spread. Instead, place 175g (6oz) chopped dates in a small pan with the zest and juice of 1 lemon and 2tbsp water. Simmer very gently for about 4 minutes or until tender. There should be very little liquid left. Leave to cool slightly. Blend one roughly chopped banana with the mixture in stage 4; fold in the date mixture. Complete as above.

Teatime Cherry Cake

Hands-on time: 20 minutes · Cooking time: 1½ hours, plus cooling
Serves 15: 320 cals, 16g fat (of which 9g saturates), 42g carbohydrate per serving

250g (9oz) unsalted butter, softened, plus
   extra to grease
about 225g (8oz) fresh cherries
250g (9oz) caster sugar
1½tsp vanilla extract
4 medium eggs
175g (6oz) plain flour, plus 1tbsp to coat
   cherries
175g (6oz) self-raising flour

For the icing
50g (2oz) fresh cherries
150ml (5fl oz) water
50g (2oz) icing sugar

1 Preheat the oven to 180°C (160°C fan oven) mark 4. Grease a 900g (2lb) loaf tin and baseline with greaseproof paper. Halve and pit the 225g (8oz) cherries and leave to dry on kitchen paper.

2 Cream the butter and caster sugar together with the vanilla extract. Add the eggs, one at a time, beating them in well after each addition.

3 Sift the plain flour with the self-raising flour and gently fold into the mixture. Toss the cut cherries in the 1tbsp plain flour and fold them carefully into the cake mixture. Spoon the mixture into the prepared tin.

4 Bake for about 1½ hours or until golden and a skewer inserted into the centre comes out clean. Cover loosely with foil if necessary. Cool in the tin for about 5 minutes, then turn out on to a wire rack to cool completely.

5 To make the icing, put the cherries in a small pan with the water and simmer for about 5 minutes or until soft. Drain, then push them through a nylon sieve to produce about 50ml (2fl oz) juice. Mix with the icing sugar, then drizzle over the cooled cake. Leave to set, then cut into thick slices and serve.

COOK'S TIPS: Buy the best-quality fruit available, avoiding any that are split or diseased. Good quality cherries can be kept covered in the fridge for about ten days.

Cherry and Almond Muffins

Hands-on: 10 minutes · Cooking time: 25 minutes, plus cooling

Serves 12: 190 cals, 6g fat (of which trace saturates), 33g carbohydrate per serving

225g (8oz) plain flour
1tsp baking powder
pinch of salt
75g (3oz) caster sugar
50g (2oz) ground almonds
300ml (10fl oz) milk
3tbsp lemon juice

50ml (2fl oz) sunflower oil or melted butter
1 large egg
1tsp almond extract
350g (12oz) glacé cherries, preferably natural
   coloured
roughly crushed sugar cubes to decorate
soft cheese and honey to serve

1 Preheat the oven to 190°C (170°C fan oven) mark 5. Line a muffin tin with 12 muffin cases.

2 Sift together the flour, baking powder and salt. Add the sugar and ground almonds.

3 Whisk together the milk, lemon juice, oil or butter, the egg and almond extract.

4 Roughly chop the glacé cherries and add to the dry ingredients. Pour in the liquid mixture. Stir the mixture together until all the ingredients are just combined – it should look lumpy. Do not overmix or the muffins will be tough.

5 Spoon the mixture evenly into the muffin cases. Sprinkle with the crushed sugar cubes and bake for about 25 minutes until well risen and golden.

6 Leave the muffins to cool in the tin for 5 minutes, then complete cooling on a wire rack. These muffins are best eaten on the day of making, accompanied by soft cheese and honey.

FRUIT INDULGENCE

Who needs chocolate when you have luscious and juicy fruit? These mouthwatering combinations below offer fresh and comforting desserts. The mix of cardamom seeds and saffron strands in the Mango and Cardamom Gateau adds a subtle fragrance to the sponge. The Crumbly Fruit and Nut Pie is delicious – the fruit juices flow into a mixture of lemon, spice, brown sugar and butter.

Apple and Pecan Meringue Cake

Apple Shorties

Apple Rock Cakes

Spiced Apple Pastry

Apple Flan

Crumbly Fruit and Nut Pie

Apricot and Almond Traybake

Banoffi Fudge Pie

Strawberry Pavlova

Mango and Cardamom Gateau

Cherry Cake

Apple and Pecan Meringue Cake

Hands-on time: 45 minutes · Cooking time: 1½-2 hours, plus cooling

Serves 10-12: 500–370 cals, 36–24g fat (of which 11–10g saturates), 38–36g carbohydrate per serving

125g (4oz) caster sugar
175g (6oz) light muscovado sugar
4 large egg whites
125g (4oz) pecan nuts, roughly chopped
2tsp ground cinnamon
700g (1½lb) cooking apples
zest and juice of 1 lemon

450g (1lb) eating apples, such as Cox
  or Braeburn
50g (2oz) unsalted butter
oil, to grease
284ml carton double cream
142ml tub fromage frais
icing sugar and cinnamon to dust

1 Preheat the oven to 150°C (130°C fan oven) mark 2. Line two baking sheets with non-stick baking parchment and draw a 28cm (11in) diameter circle on each. Turn the paper over so that the pencil mark is underneath. Sieve together the caster sugar and 125g (4oz) light muscovado sugar, making sure there are no lumps.

2 Whisk the egg whites until they form stiff peaks. Gradually whisk in the mixed sugars, 1tbsp at a time, keeping the meringue mixture smooth and shiny. Gently fold in three-quarters of the chopped nuts and the cinnamon. Using two dessertspoons, shape the meringue into ovals; using the circle as a guide, arrange about 16 ovals in a round, on one baking sheet. Sprinkle with the remaining chopped nuts. Spread the remaining meringue into a round on the second baking sheet. Bake for 1½–2 hours or until firm. When quite cold, peel off the parchment and store the meringues in an airtight container.

3 Meanwhile, peel, quarter, core and chop the cooking apples. Simmer in a pan with the lemon zest and juice and 50ml (2fl oz) water until softened. Peel, core and cut the eating apples into 5mm (¼in) thick slices. Melt the butter in a large frying pan over a low heat. Stir in the rest of the muscovado sugar. Increase the heat slightly and sauté the apple slices until they caramelise, about 5 minutes. Remove the apple from the pan and cool on lightly oiled foil.

4 Spoon the apple purée over the flat base. Whisk the cream into the fromage frais and spoon over the purée. Place the meringue ring on top and fill with apple slices and any remaining caramel. Dust with icing sugar and cinnamon.

Apple Shorties

Hands-on time: 20 minutes · Cooking time: 30 minutes, plus cooling

Serves 16: 100 cals, 4g fat (of which 2g saturates), 16g carbohydrate per serving

75g (3oz) unsalted butter, softened, plus
    extra to grease
40g (1½oz) caster sugar
75g (3oz) plain flour, sifted
40g (1½oz) fine semolina

1 cooking apple, about 175g (6oz)
125g (4oz) sultanas
½tsp mixed spice
2tbsp light muscovado sugar
1tsp lemon juice

1 Preheat the oven to 190°C (170°C fan oven) mark 5. Grease a 18cm (7in) square shallow baking tin. Beat together the first four ingredients until the mixture is blended. Press the mixture into the prepared tin and level the surface. Bake for 15 minutes.

2 Meanwhile, peel and grate the apple and mix with the remaining ingredients. Spoon evenly over the shortbread and return to the oven for a further 15 minutes. Cool for a few minutes, then cut into 16 squares. Leave to cool completely, then remove from the tin.

Apple Rock Cakes

Hands-on time: 10 minutes · Cooking time: 30 minutes

Serves 12: 290 cals, 13g fat (of which 8g saturates), 40g carbohydrate per serving

175g (6oz) plain wholemeal flour, sifted
175g (6oz) plain white flour, sifted
2tsp baking powder
½tsp grated nutmeg
¼tsp mixed spice
125g (4oz) light muscovado sugar

175g (6oz) unsalted butter, plus extra to grease
125g (4oz) dried stoned dates, chopped
1 cooking apple, about 175g (6oz), peeled
    and grated
1 medium egg
2–4tbsp milk

1 Preheat the oven to 190°C (170°C fan oven) mark 5. Grease two baking sheets. In a bowl, mix together the wholemeal flour, plain flour, baking powder, nutmeg, spice and sugar. Rub in the butter.

2 Stir in the dates, apple, egg and enough milk until the mixture forms a soft dough. Place large spoonfuls of the dough on to the baking sheets. Bake for about 20 minutes. Cool before placing on to wire racks.

Spiced Apple Pastry

Hands-on time: 25 minutes · Cooking time: 1 hour 20 minutes

Serves 8: 490 cals, 27g fat (of which 15g saturates), 58g carbohydrate per serving

225g (8oz) puff pastry, see page 14
175g (6oz) unsalted butter, softened
125g (4oz) caster sugar
50g (2oz) light muscovado sugar
3 medium eggs
3tbsp cider

1tsp mixed spice
175g (6oz) self-raising flour, plus extra for
    rolling out
4 Granny Smith apples
lemon juice to brush
icing sugar to dust

1 Preheat the oven to 200°C (180°C fan oven) mark 6.

2 Thinly roll out the pastry on a lightly floured surface. Place on a baking sheet and prick all over with a fork. Bake for 10–12 minutes or until well risen and golden. Cool.

3 Meanwhile, cream together the butter and sugars until very pale. Beat in the eggs with the cider (the mixture will curdle). Fold in the mixed spice and flour. Peel, core and roughly chop one apple and fold into the cake mixture.

4 Trim the cooked pastry to fit the bottom of a 28 × 18cm (11 × 7in) shallow cake tin. Spoon the cake mixture evenly over the pastry base and level the surface.

5 Peel, core and halve the remaining apples. Thinly slice each half and press down into the cake mixture. Brush lightly with lemon juice.

6 Reduce the oven temperature to 180°C (160°C fan oven) mark 4 and bake for about 1 hour 10 minutes or until firm to the touch. Dust with icing sugar and serve warm on its own or with Butterscotch Sauce (see page 17) and vanilla ice cream.

Apple Flan

Hands-on time: 1 hour, plus chilling · Cooking time: 1 hour 20 minutes
Serves 6–8: 470–350 cals, 30–22g fat (of which 16–12g saturates), 49–37g carbohydrate per serving

For the puff pastry
90g (3½oz) unsalted butter, at room
    temperature
100g (3½oz) plain flour
pinch of salt

For the filling
50g (2oz) unsalted butter, softened
50g (2oz) caster sugar
1 medium egg, beaten
40g (1½oz) ground almonds

For the apple purée
450g (1lb) cooking apples
25g (1oz) unsalted butter
1tbsp caster sugar

To finish
3 eating apples, about 450g (1lb) total weight
lemon juice
15g (½oz) unsalted butter, melted
1–2tbsp demerara sugar
5tbsp apricot jam

1 First make the pastry (see Puff Pastry, page 14).

2 To prepare the filling, cream the butter and sugar together until light and fluffy. Add the beaten egg, a little at a time. Fold in the almonds. Cover and chill until required.

3 Prepare the apple purée: peel, quarter, core and chop the cooking apples. Place in a small pan and add the butter and sugar. Cover and cook until the apples are softened (about 10 minutes). Sieve, cool, cover and chill until required.

4 Preheat the oven to 220°C (200°C fan oven) mark 7. Roll the pastry out and use to line a 23cm (9in) base measurement, loose-based, fluted flan tin. Prick the base all over with a fork, then freeze for 15 minutes. Line the pastry with a piece of foil, folding it down carefully over the outside of the flan case. Fill with baking-blind beans (see page 15). Bake at for 15 minutes. Remove the foil and beans, prick the pastry base again, then bake at 180°C (160°C fan oven) mark 4 for a further 15–20 minutes or until the pastry is well browned. Cool.

5 Meanwhile, peel, quarter, core and slice the eating apples and toss in lemon juice to prevent them from discolouring. Spread the almond cream over the base of the cool flan and top with the apple purée. Arrange the apple slices over the flan, brush with melted butter and sprinkle over the sugar.

6 Bake at 190°C (170° fan oven) mark 5 for about 35 minutes. Ease out of the tin and place on a serving platter. Warm the apricot jam with 1tbsp water. Sieve and then brush all over the flan. Serve the flan warm.

Crumbly Fruit and Nut Pie

Hands-on time: 20 minutes · Cooking time: 55 minutes

Serves 6: 500 cals, 30g fat (of which 13g saturates), 52g carbohydrate per serving

350g (12oz) shortcrust pastry, see page 14
beaten egg to glaze
75g (3oz) mixed whole nuts
40g (1½oz) butter, chilled and cubed
40g (1½oz) demerara sugar
350g (12oz) gooseberries
225g (8oz) blackberries, tayberries or
loganberries

2tbsp plain flour, sifted, plus extra for
rolling out
4tbsp caster sugar
zest of 1 lemon
½tsp ground ginger or mixed spice
thin custard to accompany (optional)

1 Line a 23cm (9in) metal pie plate with about three-quarters of the pastry. Reserve the trimmings. Chill, then bake blind (see page 15). Cool.

2 To decorate the edge of the pie, roll out the pastry trimmings to a thickness of 3mm (⅛in). Put on a baking sheet and chill, then cut into leaf shapes. Brush the edge of the cold baked shell with beaten egg and lay the leaves around the edge to form a wreath. Chill, then glaze again. Bake at 190°C (170°C fan oven) mark 5 and bake the pastry for about 10 minutes or until lightly coloured.

3 Roughly chop the nuts, preferably in a food processor, add the cubed butter and demerara sugar and whiz for 10 seconds only. Set aside. Pick over the fruit and wash, if necessary, then drain well.

4 Mix the flour with the caster sugar, lemon zest and ground ginger or mixed spice. Sprinkle half on the bottom of the pie. Toss the remaining flour mixture with the fruit and pile into the pie. Sprinkle the nut mixture on top.

5 Bake at 190°C (170°C fan oven) mark 5 for about 25 minutes or until the fruit are beginning to soften and release their juices, and the nuts are brown. Serve immediately accompanied by thin custard, if you like.

Apricot and Almond Traybake

Hands-on time: 20 minutes · Cooking time: 30–40 minutes, plus cooling

Serves 18: 280 cals, 16g fat (of which 8g saturates), 30g carbohydrate per serving

250g (9oz) unsalted butter, softened, plus
    extra to grease
225g (8oz) golden caster sugar
275g (10oz) self-raising flour, sifted
2tsp baking powder
finely grated zest of 1 orange and 2tbsp
    orange juice

75g (3oz) ground almonds
5 medium eggs, lightly beaten
225g (8oz) ready-to-eat dried aprocots,
    roughly chopped
25g (1oz) flaked almonds
icing sugar to dust (optional)

1 Preheat the oven to 180°C (160°C fan oven) mark 4. Grease a 20.5 x 33cm (8 x 13in) roasting tin and baseline with greaseproof paper.

2 Put the butter, caster sugar, flour, baking powder, orange zest, ground almonds and eggs into the bowl of a large freestanding mixer. Cover the bowl with a clean teatowel to stop the flour shooting everywhere and mix on a low setting for 30 seconds, then increase the speed and mix for 1 minute until thoroughly combined.

3 Remove the bowl from the mixer. Fold in the dried apricots with a large metal spoon. Spoon the mixture into the prepared tin, then smooth the surface of the mixture with a palette knife and sprinkle the flaked almonds over the top

4 Bake for 30–40 minutes or until risen and golden brown. It's ready when a skewer inserted into the centre comes out clean.

5 Cool in the tin, then cut into 18 bars. Dust with icing sugar, if liked.

Banoffi Fudge Pie

Hands-on time: 40 minutes · Cooking time: 25 minutes, plus cooling

Serves 6–8: 780–580 cals, 51–37g fat (of which 29–22g saturates), 76–57g carbohydrate per serving

flour for rolling out
250g (9oz) shortcrust pastry, see page 14
75g (3oz) unsalted butter
50g (2oz) light muscovado sugar
2tbsp milk

220g can condensed milk
5 medium-size bananas
284ml carton double cream
lemon juice
50g (2oz) caster sugar

1 Preheat the oven to 200°C (180°C fan oven) mark 6. Roll out the pastry on a lightly floured surface and use to line a 2.5cm (1in) deep, 23cm (9in) round loose-base flan tin. Bake blind until light golden and dried out (see page 15). Remove from the oven and leave to cool.

2 Put the butter and muscovado sugar in a small, heavy-based pan. Heat gently until the butter melts and the sugar dissolves. Bring to the boil and bubble for 1 minute only, stirring frequently. Off the heat, add the milk and condensed milk, bring to the boil and bubble for
2 minutes only or until the mixture thickens to the consistency of a very thick sauce and turns golden. Stir constantly or the mixture will burn. Keep warm.

3 Meanwhile, thickly slice four of the bananas and place in the pastry case. Spoon the warm fudge thinly but evenly over the bananas to cover completely. Leave to cool, then chill until set, about 45 minutes.

4 Whisk the cream until it just holds its shape. Pile the cream in the centre of the pie. Chill for at least 1 hour, so that the caramel will set immediately on it. Slice the remaining banana and coat with lemon juice. Pile on top of the cream.

5 Put the caster sugar in a small, heavy-based pan. Heat gently until the sugar dissolves and turns a golden caramel colour. Cool for about 1 minute or until the caramel thickens and darkens slightly, then spoon over the banana. (The caramel will run through the cream.) Chill immediately to set. The pie will hold up in the fridge for 2–3 hours. Leave at room temperature for 30 minutes before serving.

COOK'S TIP: If you prefer a thicker toffee fudge layer, increase the filling ingredients to 175g (6oz) butter and 125g (4oz) light muscovado sugar and bubble for 1 minute. Then add 4tbsp milk and 405g can condensed milk and bubble for about 3–4 minutes. Use only 3 bananas in the base. Complete as above.

Strawberry Pavlova

Hands–on time: 20 minutes · Cooking time: 1¼ hours, plus cooling

Serves 6: 500 cals, 31g fat (of which 17g saturates), 52g carbohydrate per serving

4 medium egg whites
225g (8oz) golden caster sugar
1tbsp cornflour
1tbsp vanilla extract
2tsp white wine vinegar

450g (1lb) strawberries
3tbsp framboise (raspberry liqueur)
284ml carton double cream
200g tub half-fat crème fraîche

1 Preheat the oven to 130°C (110°C fan oven) mark ½. Draw a 20.5cm (8in) circle on to non-stick baking parchment, turn over (so ink is underneath) and put on a baking sheet.

2 Whisk the egg whites until they form stiff peaks. Continue to whisk the egg whites and start to add the sugar, 1tbsp at a time, until the meringue is stiff and glossy – this will take around 5 minutes. Add the cornflour, vanilla extract and vinegar and whisk briefly for around 1 minute to combine. This will soften the mixture slightly.

3 Put a little meringue in each corner of the baking sheet to secure the parchment, then use a metal spoon to dollop the meringue on to the marked circle. Use a palette knife to make a slight dip in the centre. Bake for 1¼ hours until firm at the edges and slightly soft in the centre. Cool.

4 To prepare the strawberries, put the fruit in a colander and dip into a sink of clean water to rinse. Pat dry gently with kitchen paper, then remove the stalks. Halve the fruit if they're large, then put in a bowl and add the framboise. Toss together until the strawberries are coated, then set aside to macerate.

5 Pour the double cream into a clean bowl and whip until softly peaking, then add the crème fraîche and fold together until a thick consistency forms. Use a palette knife to remove the pavlova from the baking parchment and put it on a serving plate.

6 Add three-quarters of the macerated strawberries to the cream and crème fraîche mixture and fold together gently. Spoon into the pavlova to fill the middle, decorate with the remaining strawberries and drizzle over any juice.

Mango and Cardamom Gateau

Hands-on time: 45 minutes · Cooking time: 25–30 minutes, plus cooling

Serves 10: 310 cals, 16g fat (of which 8g saturates), 39g carbohydrate per serving

For the sponge
50g (2oz) unsalted butter, plus extra
    to grease
4 green cardamom pods
good pinch of saffron strands
4 large eggs
125g (4oz) caster sugar
100g (3½oz) plain flour

To complete
142ml carton double cream
150g (5oz) Greek yogurt
3tbsp icing sugar, plus extra to dust
2 large ripe mangoes
4tbsp orange juice
shredded orange to decorate

1 Preheat the oven to 180°C (160°C fan oven) mark 4. Grease two 18cm (7in) sandwich tins, or one deep 18cm (7in) round cake tin and baseline with greaseproof papper

2 Split the cardamom pods and remove the black seeds. Crush the seeds to a powder with the saffron strands. Put the butter into a pan and heat gently until melted, then remove from the heat and leave to cool slightly for a few minutes until beginning to thicken.

3 Put the eggs and caster sugar into a large heatproof bowl and whisk until evenly blended, using an electric whisk. Put the bowl over a pan of hot water and whisk until pale and thick enough to leave a trail on the surface when the whisk is lifted. Remove the bowl from the pan and whisk until cool and thick.

4 Sift the spices and flour together. Fold half into the whisked mixture with a large metal spoon or plastic spatula. Pour the cooled butter around the edge of the mixture, leaving the sediment behind. Gradually fold it in very lightly, cutting through the mixture until it is all incorporated. Carefully fold in the remaining flour as lightly as possible. Pour into the prepared tins. Bake for 25–30 minutes, until well risen and the cakes spring back when lightly pressed. Loosen the cake edge and leave in the tins for 5 minutes.

5 For the filling, whip the cream until it holds its shape. Stir in the yogurt with 2tbsp icing sugar to make the cream mixture for the filling. Sandwich the cake with the cream mixture and one sliced mango. Refrigerate for 2–3 hours, dust with icing sugar and decorate with shredded orange slices just before serving.

6 Liquidise the remaining mango flesh with 1tbsp icing sugar and the orange juice; pass through a nylon sieve to remove all the fibres. Cover and chill. Serve with the gateau.

Cherry Cake

Hands-on time: 10 minutes · Cooking time: 1 hour 10 minutes, plus cooling

Serves 8: 310 cals, 21g fat (of which 12g saturates), 24g carbohydrate per serving

175g (6oz) unsalted butter, softened, plus
    extra to grease
175g (6oz) plain white flour
2tsp baking powder
pinch of salt
175g (6oz) caster sugar, plus extra to dust

½tsp vanilla extract
zest of 1 lemon
3 medium eggs, beaten
milk
225g (8oz) small fresh cherries, stoned

1 Preheat the oven to 190°C (170°C fan oven) mark 5. Grease a 900g (2lb) loaf tin and baseline with greaseproof paper.

2 Sift the flour with the baking powder and salt. Cream together the butter and sugar until pale and fluffy. Gradually beat in the vanilla extract, lemon zest and eggs. Gently fold in the flour. Add a small amount of milk, if the mixture seems a little stiff. Fold in the stoned cherries.

3 Turn the mixture into the prepared tin and bake for about 1 hour 10 minutes, or until risen, well browned and slightly shrunk away from the sides of the tin. Cover lightly with foil, if necessary, to prevent overbrowning.

4 Cool in the tin for about 10 minutes, then turn out on to a rack to complete the cooling. Store wrapped, in the fridge, and dust with caster sugar to serve.

TORTES AND TARTS

Whether you make a rich and creamy torte or a tasty pastry tart, with delicious fillings of fruit, chocolate, cheese or nuts, you can't fail to please. Seduce your friends with the special Strawberry Chocolate Tart and watch as they devour the spectacular Tiramisu Torte.

Fudge Nut Tart

Lemon Fudge Tart

Tiramisu Torte

Chocolate Orange Torte

Walnut and Apple Tart

Crème Brûlée Tart

Raspberry and Vanilla Custard Tart

Strawberry Chocolate Tart

Sweet Ricotta Tart

Fudge Nut Tart

Hands-on time: 20 minutes · Cooking time: 50 minutes

Serves 8: 720 cals, 62g fat (of which 23g saturates), 35g carbohydrate per serving

225g (8oz) unsalted butter
175g (6oz) plain flour, sifted, plus extra for
   rolling out
25g (1oz) caster sugar
125g (4oz) skinned hazelnuts
125g (4oz) pecan nuts

75g (3oz) light muscovado sugar
150ml (5fl oz) double cream
zest and juice of 1 lemon
1 medium egg, beaten
whole pecan nuts to decorate
2tbsp warmed apricot jam to glaze

1 Preheat the oven to 200°C (180°C fan oven) mark 6. Cut 125g (4oz) butter into small pieces and rub into the flour until the mixture looks like fine breadcrumbs. Stir in the caster sugar and bind to a dough with 2–3tbsp water. Roll out on a lightly floured surface and use to line a 23cm (9in) fluted flan tin or a 34 × 11cm (13½ × 4½in) loose-base, fluted tranche tin. Bake blind until golden and well dried out (see page 15).

2 Meanwhile, toast the nuts until lightly browned. Cool and then roughly chop. Warm the remaining butter with the muscovado sugar and cream until evenly mixed.

3 Cool slightly, then stir in the chopped nuts, lemon zest, 2tbsp lemon juice and the beaten egg. Mix well.

4 Pour the mixture into the tart case and arrange the whole pecan nuts on top. Reduce the oven temperature to 180°C (160°C fan oven) mark 4 and bake for 25–30 minutes or until lightly set.

5 Brush the tart evenly with the warm apricot jam to glaze.

Lemon Fudge Tart

Hands-on time: 25 minutes, plus chilling · Cooking time: 1 hour 50 minutes to 2 hours 10 minutes

Serves 20: 230 cals, 14g fat (of which 7g saturates), 23g carbohydrate per serving

175g (6oz) plain flour, sifted
1tbsp icing sugar, plus extra to dust
265g (9½oz) unsalted butter
zest and juice of 5 lemons, about
    200ml (7fl oz)

10 medium eggs
275g (10oz) caster sugar

1 Preheat the oven to 170°C (150°C fan oven) mark 3.

2 Whiz together the flour, icing sugar and 100g (3½oz) of the butter in a food processor until the mixture looks like breadcrumbs. Divide between two 22cm (8½in) ceramic flan dishes and press into the base using your fingertips. Bake for 35–40 minutes until golden.

3 Melt the remaining butter for the filling and place in a processor with the lemon zest and juice, eggs and caster sugar. Whiz until smooth, then pour over the warm shortbread. (The base must be warm when the filling is put in or the pastry crumbs will rise to the surface.)

4 Reduce the oven temperature to 130°C (110°C fan oven) mark ½ and bake the tart for 1¼–1½ hours or until just set. (The slower the cooking time, the smoother the texture.) Leave to cool, then chill in the fridge for up to four days.

5 To serve, remove from the fridge for 1 hour. Cut into wedges, ease out of the dishes and dust heavily with icing sugar. Return to the fridge until required.

Tiramisu Torte

Hands-on time: 40 minutes, plus chilling · Cooking time: 45 minutes, plus cooling

Serves 8–10: 870–690 cals, 60–48g fat (of which 35–28g saturates), 73–58g carbohydrate per serving

275g (10oz) amaretti biscuits, ratafias or macaroons
75g (3oz) unsalted butter
700g (1½lb) mascarpone or Philadelphia cream cheese (at room temperature)
150g (5oz) caster sugar
3 medium eggs, separated

25g (1oz) plain flour, sifted
3tbsp dark rum
½tsp vanilla extract
175g (6oz) plain chocolate
1tbsp finely ground coffee
3tbsp Tia Maria or other coffee liqueur

1 Put the biscuits in a blender or food processor and whiz until finely ground. Melt the butter and stir in the crumbs until well coated. Spoon into a 23cm (9in) spring-release cake tin. Using the back of a spoon, press evenly over the base and 4cm (1½in) up the sides to form a shell. Chill for at least 30 minutes or until firm.

2 Preheat the oven to 200°C (180°C fan oven) mark 6. Using a wooden spoon or in an electric mixer, beat the cheese until smooth. Add the sugar and beat again until smooth, then beat in the egg yolks. Stir the flour, rum and vanilla extract into half the mixture.

3 Melt the chocolate (see page 13), cool slightly, then stir in the coffee and coffee liqueur. Stir into the remaining half of the cheese mixture. Whisk the egg whites until they form soft peaks, then fold half the egg whites into each flavoured cheese mixture.

4 Quickly spoon alternate mounds of the two mixtures into the biscuit case until full. Using a knife, swirl them together for a marbled effect.

5 Bake for 45 minutes, covering with foil if it seems to be over-browning. At this stage the torte will be soft in the middle. Leave in the switched-off oven with the door slightly ajar, to cool; it will firm up during this time. Chill for several hours.

Chocolate Orange Torte

Hands-on time: 30 minutes · Cooking time: 55-60 minutes, plus cooling

Serves 12: 290 cals, 18g fat (of which 6g saturates), 25g carbohydrate per serving

75g (3oz) unsalted butter, diced, plus extra
   to grease
100g (3½oz) dark chocolate (at least 70%
   cocoa solids), broken into pieces

6 medium eggs
225g (8oz) golden caster sugar
150g (5oz) ground almonds, sifted
zest and juice of 1 orange

1 Preheat the oven to 190°C (170°C fan oven) mark 5. Grease a 20.5cm (8in) spring-release cake tin and line with greaseproof paper.

2 Melt the chocolate and butter (see page 13). Remove the bowl from the pan and put to one side to cool a little.

3 Put the eggs and sugar in a large bowl and mix with an electric whisk until the volume has tripled and the mixture is thick and foamy – it'll take around 5–10 minutes.

4 Add the ground almonds and orange zest and juice to the egg mixture, then gently fold together with a metal spoon.

5 Pour around two-thirds of the mixture into the prepared tin. Add the melted chocolate and butter to the remaining mixture and fold together. Add to the tin and swirl around just once or twice to create a marbled effect.

6 Bake for 50 minutes to 1 hour. Leave to cool in the tin, then carefully remove the torte and slice.

Walnut and Apple Tart

Hands-on time: 25 minutes, plus chilling · Cooking time: 1 hour 5 minutes
Serves 8: 620 cals, 37g fat (of which 19g saturates), 66g carbohydrate per serving

For the pastry
225g (8oz) plain flour
2tbsp golden icing sugar
125g (4oz) unsalted butter, chilled and diced
1 medium egg, beaten

For the filling
200g (7oz) runny honey
125g (4oz) unsalted butter, softened

125g (4oz) light muscovado sugar
3 medium eggs, beaten
zest and juice of 1 lemon
125g (4oz) walnuts, roughly chopped
125g (4oz) ready-to-eat dried apples and
    pears, roughly chopped, plus 3 dried pear
    slices to decorate
crème fraîche to serve

1 To make the pastry, put the flour and icing sugar into the bowl of a food processor. Add the diced butter and whiz until the mixture looks like fine breadcrumbs. Add the egg and 1tbsp cold water and pulse until the mixture just starts to come together. Tip the pastry on to a clean worksurface and knead it briefly to form a ball. Wrap in clingfilm and chill for 30 minutes.

2 For the filling, warm 175g (6oz) honey in a small pan over a low heat. Put the softened butter in a large bowl with the muscovado sugar. Using an electric hand whisk, mix together until light and fluffy. Add the eggs, lemon zest and juice, walnuts, chopped apples and pears and warm honey. Stir well and set aside.

3 Put the pastry between two sheets of greaseproof paper and roll out thinly. Peel off and discard the top sheet of paper, then flip over and put the pastry into a 23cm (9in) loose-base tart tin. Peel off the paper and set aside. Ease the pastry into the tin and trim the edge, then prick the base with a fork. Cover with clingfilm and chill for 30 minutes.

4 Preheat the oven to 180°C (160°C fan oven) mark 4. Put the reserved greaseproof paper in the tart case, fill with baking beans and bake for 10–15 minutes. Remove the paper and beans and bake the pastry for a further 5 minutes until golden. Pour in the walnut and apple filling and arrange the pear slices on top. Brush with the remaining honey.

5 Put the tart on a baking sheet, cover it with foil and bake for 20 minutes. Remove the foil and bake for a further 25 minutes until the tart is golden brown and slightly risen. Cool it in the tin, then remove, put on a plate and serve with crème fraîche.

Crème Brûlée Tart

Hands-on time: 30 minutes, plus chilling and freezing · Cooking time: 45 minutes

Serves 8: 990 cals, 81g fat (of which 44g saturates), 62g carbohydrate per serving

225g (8oz) plain flour, sifted, plus extra for
    rolling out
125g (4oz) unsalted butter, in pieces
200g (7oz) caster sugar
10 large egg yolks
1 large egg white

50g (2oz) stem ginger, about 3 balls, drained
    and finely chopped
900ml (1½ pints) double cream
granulated sugar for brûléeing
physalis to serve (optional)

1 Put the flour, butter, 125g (4oz) caster sugar and 4 egg yolks in a food processor and whiz until the mixture forms a ball. Wrap in clingfilm and leave to rest in the fridge for 30 minutes.

2 Roll out the pastry on a lightly floured surface to 5mm (¼in) thick and line a 4cm (1½in) deep, 23cm (9in) loose-base fluted flan tin. (This is a rich pastry so work quickly.) Freeze, uncovered, for 1 hour.

3 Preheat the oven to 190°C (170°C fan oven) mark 5. Remove the flan case from the freezer, line with foil and fill with baking beans. Bake for 20–25 minutes. Remove the foil and beans and return to the oven to dry out completely, keeping the pastry loosely covered with a tent of foil. Cook until golden brown all over, about 5 minutes. Paint with the egg white and return to the oven for a further 2 minutes. Leave to cool.

4 Beat together the remaining egg yolks and caster sugar. Put the stem ginger in a pan with the cream. Bring up to barely simmering point and pour through a sieve on to the egg yolk and sugar mixture. Stir well.

5 Scatter the ginger pieces over the pastry case. Return the custard to the pan and, over a gentle heat, bring *almost* to the boil, stirring all the time (this will take about 10 minutes). As soon as the custard shows signs of boiling, pour though a sieve straight into the pastry case. Leave to cool, then refrigerate, uncovered, overnight.

6 Sprinkle the filling evenly with granulated sugar and, using a blow torch, brûlée the sugar. Alternatively, caramelise the sugar under the grill. Refrigerate for 2–3 hours.

7 To serve, remove the flan tin, cut the tart into wedges and decorate with a physalis, if you like.

Raspberry and Vanilla Custard Tart

Hands-on time: 40 minutes, plus cooling · Cooking time: around 1 hour

Serves 6: 510 cals, 37g fat (of which 21g saturates), 39g carbohydrate per serving

175g (6oz) plain flour, sifted
125g (4oz) unsalted butter, in pieces, plus extra to grease
25g (1oz) vanilla sugar (see Cook's Tip), or ¼tsp vanilla extract
1tsp orange zest

2 medium eggs, plus 3 egg yolks
40g (1½oz) caster sugar
½ vanilla pod
450ml (15fl oz) single cream
175g (6oz) fresh raspberries
vanilla sugar or icing sugar to dust

1 To make the pastry, whiz together the flour and butter in a food processor. Add the vanilla sugar or extract, the orange zest, one egg yolk and 2–3tsp cold water. Whiz to a stiff dough, then wrap in clingfilm and chill in the fridge for about 20 minutes. Grease a 4cm (1½in) deep, 20cm (8in) loose-base fluted flan tin.

2 Roll out the dough on a lightly floured surface and line the flan tin, then chill again for 20 minutes. Preheat the oven to 200°C (180°C fan oven) mark 6. Bake blind for 20–25 minutes (see page 15).

3 Meanwhile, make the custard filling. Put the whole eggs, remaining egg yolks and the caster sugar in a bowl and beat well. Split the vanilla pod, scrape out the seeds and put both in a pan with the cream. Cook over a very low heat until the cream is well flavoured and almost boiling. Pour on to the egg mixture, whisking constantly; strain into the pastry case.

4 Reduce the oven temperature to 150°C (130°C fan oven) mark 2 and bake the tart for 45 minutes or until the centre is lightly set. Remove from the oven and leave until cold.

5 Remove the tart from the tin and arrange the raspberries on top. Dust with vanilla or icing sugar to serve.

COOK'S TIP: To make your own vanilla sugar, store one or two vanilla pods in an airtight jar of caster sugar. (Use pods where you have scraped out the seeds.) After a couple of days the sugar will be ready. Just top up the sugar as you use it – no need to replace the vanilla pod.

Strawberry Chocolate Tart

Hands-on time: 30 minutes, plus chilling · Cooking time: 45 minutes

Serves 6–8: 900–690 cals, 59–44g fat (of which 33–25g saturates), 80–60g carbohydrate per serving

4 medium eggs, plus 2 egg yolks
225g (8oz) plain flour, sifted, plus extra for
    rolling out
275g (10oz) unsalted butter
50g (2oz) icing sugar
zest and juice of 1–2 oranges

225g (8oz) plain chocolate, finely chopped
75g (3oz) caster sugar
6tbsp orange liqueur, such as Grand Marnier
    or Cointreau
1tsp powdered gelatine
700g (1½lb) fresh strawberries

1 Lightly beat one egg and keep to one side. To make the pastry, whiz the flour, 150g (5oz) butter, the icing sugar and orange zest in a food processor until the mixture looks like fine breadcrumbs. Add all but 2tsp of the beaten egg and pulse until the pastry comes together in a ball. Wrap and chill for 30 minutes.

2 Roll out the dough on a lightly floured surface and line a 4cm (1½in) deep, 23cm (9in) loose-base fluted tart tin. Prick the base and chill for 30 minutes. Preheat the oven to 200°C (180°C fan oven) mark 6. Line the pastry with greaseproof paper and baking beans. Bake for 10 minutes. Remove the paper and beans and cook for 10 minutes until cooked through. Brush with the reserved egg and return to the oven for 1 minute to seal. Leave to cool slightly. Reduce the oven temperature to 190°C (170°C fan oven) mark 5.

3 To make the filling, melt the remaining butter in a pan. Off the heat, add the chocolate and stir until it is melted and smooth. In a large bowl, whisk the remaining eggs, yolks and 50g (2oz) caster sugar until pale and light. Fold in the melted chocolate and 4tbsp liqueur.

4 Pour the mixture into the pastry case and bake for 15–17 minutes, until the mousse is puffed and has formed a crust. Leave to cool in the tin. Chill for 5 hours or overnight.

5 Pour 75ml (3fl oz) orange juice into a small heatproof bowl, sprinkle over the powdered gelatine and leave to soften for 2–3 minutes. Stir the remaining liqueur and caster sugar into the juice. Place over a pan of gently simmering water until the gelatine has dissolved.

6 Fold the orange juice mixture into the strawberries, then arrange on top of the tart. Keep in the fridge until ready to serve, but for no longer than 8–10 hours.

Sweet Ricotta Tart

Hands-on time: 25 minutes, plus chilling · Cooking time: 1 hour

Serves 8: 410 cals, 14g fat (of which 8g saturates), 65g carbohydrate per serving

For the pastry
200g (7oz) plain flour, sifted, plus extra
    for rolling out
50g (2oz) golden caster sugar
75g (3oz) unsalted butter, diced and
    chilled
1 medium egg, beaten

For the filling
100g (3½oz) cracked wheat or bulgur
    wheat

200ml (7fl oz) milk
250g tub ricotta cheese
150g (5oz) golden caster sugar
2 medium eggs
1tbsp orange flower water
1tsp vanilla extract
½tsp ground cinnamon
1 piece – around 40g (1½oz) – candied peel,
    finely chopped
3tbsp apricot glaze
a little icing sugar to dust

1 To make the pastry, whiz the flour, sugar and butter in a processor until the mixture looks like breadcrumbs. Add the egg and whiz again until the mixture just comes together. You may need to add 1–2tsp cold water if it's dry. Knead briefly, then wrap in clingfilm and chill for 30 minutes.

2 To make the filling, put the cracked or bulgur wheat in a pan and add the milk, then cover and bring to the boil. Turn down the heat and simmer for 5–8 minutes until all the liquid has been absorbed. Cool.

3 Preheat the oven to 190°C (170°C fan oven) mark 5. Roll out the pastry on a lightly floured surface and use to line a 20.5cm (8in) loose-base sandwich cake tin. Cover and chill for 10 minutes. Knead together the trimmings, then wrap and store in the fridge.

4 Line the pastry with greaseproof paper and baking beans and bake blind for 10 minutes (see page 15). Remove the paper and beans and continue to bake for 4–5 minutes or until the pastry has dried out.

5 Put the ricotta in a bowl and add the sugar, eggs, orange flower water, vanilla extract and cinnamon. Beat well. Add the candied peel and cracked wheat and mix together. Roll out the ball of pastry trimmings and cut out six 1 × 20.5cm (½ × 8in) strips. Pour the filling into the pastry case and lay the strips on top. Bake for 45 minutes, then transfer to a wire rack to cool.

6 Warm the apricot glaze and brush between the pastry strips. Protecting the glazed area with greaseproof paper, dust the pastry strips with icing sugar.

BISCUITS AND BROWNIES

What could be better than the enticing aroma of a freshly baked tray of cookies? Perhaps tucking into them! The cookies are wonderfully quick to make and although the brownies take longer it's certainly worth the wait. Try the Chocolate Brownies for a tempting treat or the Millionaire's Shortbread for a rich biscuit nibble.

Peanut and Raisin Cookies

Spiced Star Biscuits

Millionaire's Shortbread

Spiced Sultana and Lemon Cookies

Shortbread Biscuits

Chocolate and Pistachio Biscotti

Chocolate Brownies

Chocolate Fudge Brownies

White Chocolate and Macadamia Nut Brownies

Sticky Pear and Chocolate Brownie Cake

Peanut and Raisin Cookies

Hands-on time: 10 minutes · Cooking time: 15 minutes, plus cooling

Serves 30: 110 cals, 6g fat (of which 3g saturates), 14g carbohydrate per serving

125g (4oz) unsalted butter, softened, plus
  extra to grease
150g (5oz) caster sugar
1 medium egg
150g (5oz) plain flour, sifted

½tsp baking powder
½tsp salt
125g (4oz) crunchy peanut butter
175g (6oz) raisins

1 Preheat the oven to 190°C (170°C fan oven) mark 5. Grease two baking sheets. Beat together all the ingredients except the raisins, until well blended. Stir in the raisins.

2 Spoon large teaspoonfuls of the mixture on to the baking sheets, leaving room to spread. Bake for about 15 minutes, or until golden brown around the edges. Cool slightly, then lift on to a wire rack to cool completely.

COOK'S TIP: Leave the chopped ingredients in chunks so the cookies retain some bite and texture.

VARIATIONS

Chocolate Nut

120 cals, 7g fat (of which 3g saturates), 13g carbohydrate per serving
Omit the peanut butter and raisins and add 1tsp vanilla extract. Stir in 175g (6oz) chocolate and 75g (3oz) roughly chopped walnuts.

Coconut and Cherry

80 cals, 5g fat (of which 3g saturates), 9g carbohydrate per serving
Omit the peanut butter and raisins, reduce the sugar to 75g (3oz) and stir in 50g (2oz) desiccated coconut and 125g (4oz) rinsed, roughly chopped glacé cherries.

Oat and Cinnamon

80 cals, 4g fat (of which 2g saturates), 11g carbohydrate per serving
Omit the peanut butter and raisins and add 1tsp vanilla extract. Stir in 1tsp ground cinnamon and 75g (3oz) rolled oats.

Spiced Star Biscuits

Hands-on time: 15 minutes, plus chilling · Cooking time: 15–20 minutes, plus cooling

Serves 35: 70 cals, 2g fat (of which trace saturates), 13g carbohydrate per serving

2tbsp runny honey
25g (1oz) unsalted butter
50g (2oz) light muscovado sugar
finely grated zest of ½ lemon
finely grated zest of ½ orange
225g (8oz) self-raising flour, plus extra for
    rolling out
1tsp ground cinnamon
1tsp ground ginger
½tsp freshly grated nutmeg

pinch of ground cloves
pinch of salt
1tbsp finely chopped candied peel
50g (2oz) ground almonds
1 large egg, beaten
1½tbsp milk

To decorate
150g (5oz) icing sugar
silver sugar balls

1 Put the honey, butter, muscovado sugar and citrus zests into a small pan and stir over a low heat until the butter has melted and the ingredients are well combined.

2 Sift the flour, spices and salt together into a bowl, then add the chopped candied peel and ground almonds. Add the melted mixture, beaten egg and milk and mix until the dough comes together. Knead the dough briefly until smooth, then wrap in clingfilm and chill for at least 4 hours, or overnight.

3 Preheat the oven to 180°C (160°C fan oven) mark 4. Roll out the dough on a lightly floured surface to a 5mm (¼in) thickness. Using a 5cm (2in) cutter, stamp out stars and put on baking sheets.

4 Bake for 15–20 minutes or until just beginning to brown at the edges. Transfer the biscuits to a wire rack to cool. Store in an airtight tin for up to one week.

5 To decorate, mix the icing sugar with 1½tbsp warm water to make a smooth icing. Coat some of the biscuits with icing and finish with a piped edging if you like, then decorate with silver balls. Pipe dots of icing on the plain biscuits and attach silver balls. Allow the icing to set, then store the biscuits in an airtight container for up to one week.

Millionaire's Shortbread

Hands-on time: 25 minutes · Cooking time: 25 minutes, plus setting

Serves 20: 300 cals, 19g fat (of which 11g saturates), 30g carbohydrate per serving

250g (9oz) plain flour, sifted, plus extra for
    kneading
75g (3oz) golden caster sugar
175g (6oz) unsalted butter, softened and
    diced, plus extra to grease

For the caramel
2 × 397g cans sweetened condensed milk
100g (3½oz) light muscovado sugar
100g (3½oz) unsalted butter

For the topping
250g (9oz) plain chocolate

1 Preheat the oven to 180°C (160°C fan oven) mark 4. Grease a 30.5 × 22cm (12 × 8½in) Swiss roll tin and line with greaseproof paper.

2 Put the flour, caster sugar and butter in a food processor and whiz until the mixture forms crumbs, then pulse a little more until it forms a ball. Turn out on to a lightly floured surface and knead to combine. Press the mixture into the prepared tin and bake for 20 minutes until firm to the touch and very pale brown.

3 For the caramel, put the condensed milk, sugar and butter into a heatproof bowl and microwave on High for 12 minutes, beating with a balloon whisk every 2–3 minutes until the mixture is thick and fudgey. Spoon on to the shortbread, smooth over and cool.

4 For the topping, melt the chocolate in a heatproof bowl in a microwave oven on Medium for 2 minutes and pour over the caramel.

5 Leave to set at room temperature, then cut into 20 squares to serve.

Spiced Sultana and Lemon Cookies

Hands–on time: 15 minutes · Cooking time: 15 minutes, plus cooling

Serves 20: 210 cals, 10g fat (of which 6g saturates), 28g carbohydrate per serving

225g (8oz) unsalted butter, softened, plus
   extra to grease
175g (6oz) golden caster sugar
2 medium eggs, lightly beaten
350g (12oz) self-raising flour, sifted

½tsp baking powder
pinch of bicarbonate of soda
1tsp ground mixed spice
150g (5oz) sultanas
finely grated zest of 2 lemons

1 Preheat the oven to 190°C (170°C fan oven) mark 5. Grease two baking sheets.

2 Put the butter and sugar in a bowl and use a hand whisk to cream together until pale and fluffy. Add the eggs, one at a time, beating well to make sure the mixture is thoroughly combined.

3 Add the flour, baking powder, bicarbonate of soda, ground mixed spice, sultanas and lemon zest to the bowl and fold everything together.

4 Take dessertspoons of the mixture and roll each into a ball. Put on the baking sheets, spacing them slightly apart. Dip a palette knife in water, then use to flatten the rounds slightly. Bake for 15 minutes.

5 Cool the cookies on a wire rack. Store the cookies in an airtight tin and eat within two days.

Shortbread Biscuits

Hands-on time: 15 minutes, plus chilling · Cooking time: 15 minutes

Serves 12: 200 cals, 12g fat (of which 8g saturates), 23g carbohydrate per serving

175g (6oz) unsalted butter, softened,
    plus extra to grease
75g (3oz) golden caster sugar

200g (7oz) plain flour, sifted, plus extra
    for rolling out
50g (2oz) cornflour
caster sugar to sprinkle

1 Cut the butter into pieces and whiz in a processor with the sugar for 1 minute until pale and fluffy. Add the flours, and whiz until the mixture just comes together. Wrap and chill for 30 minutes. Preheat the oven to 190°C (170°C fan oven) mark 5. Lightly grease a baking sheet.

2 Roll out the dough on a lightly floured surface to 1cm (½in) thick. Using a fluted cutter, cut twelve 7cm (2¾in) rounds and put on to the baking sheet. Gently press a 4cm (1½in) plain cutter into the centre of each and prick with a fork.

3 Bake for 15 minutes or until pale golden. Sprinkle with the sugar and cool on a rack. Store in an airtight tin for up to five days.

Chocolate and Pistachio Biscotti

Hands-on time: 15 minutes, plus cooling · Cooking time: around 1 hour

Serves 30: 160 cals, 7g fat (of which 3g saturates), 20g carbohydrate per serving

300g (11oz) plain flour, sifted
75g (3oz) cocoa powder
1tsp baking powder
150g (5oz) plain chocolate chips
150g (5oz) shelled pistachio nuts

pinch of salt
75g (3oz) unsalted butter, softened
225g (8oz) granulated sugar
2 large eggs, beaten
1tbsp icing sugar

1 Preheat the oven to 180°C (160°C fan oven) mark 4. Line a large baking sheet with non-stick baking parchment.

2 Mix together the flour, cocoa powder, baking powder, chocolate chips, pistachio nuts and salt.

3 Using an electric whisk, beat together the butter and granulated sugar until light and fluffy. Gradually whisk in the beaten eggs.

4 Stir the dry ingredients into the mixture until it forms a stiff dough. With floured hands, shape the dough into two slightly flattened logs, each about 30.5 × 5cm (12 × 2in). Sprinkle with icing sugar.

5 Put the logs on to the prepared baking sheet and bake for 40–45 minutes or until they are slightly firm to the touch.

6 Cool the logs on the baking sheet for 10 minutes, then cut diagonally into 2cm (¾in) thick slices. Arrange them, cut side down, on the baking sheet and bake again for 15 minutes or until crisp. Cool on a wire rack.

Chocolate Brownies

Hands-on time: 25 minutes · Cooking time: 1 hour, plus cooling

Serves 9: 420 cals, 30g fat (of which 13g saturates), 35g carbohydrate per serving

150g (5oz) unsalted butter, plus extra to
   grease
150g (5oz) plain chocolate
1½tsp instant coffee granules
150g (5oz) caster sugar

3 medium eggs, separated
65g (2½oz) ground almonds
75g (3oz) walnuts
65g (2½oz) cornflour

1 Preheat the oven to 180°C (160°C fan oven) mark 4. Grease an 18cm (7in) square cake tin and line with greaseproof paper. Melt the chocolate and coffee (see page 13). Leave to cool slightly.

2 Cream the butter and sugar, then beat in the egg yolks, one at a time. Fold in the almonds, walnuts, cornflour and melted chocolate mix. Whisk the egg whites until they form soft peaks and fold in gently.

3 Pour the mixture into the prepared tin and bake for about 55 minutes. Cover with greaseproof paper after 30 minutes. It is cooked when a skewer inserted into the centre comes out clean.

4 Leave in the tin for 10 minutes, then turn out on to a wire rack to cool. The brownies will keep for two to three days.

Chocolate Fudge Brownies

Hands-on time: 20 minutes · Cooking time: 1 hour, plus cooling

Serves 12: 190 cals, 5g fat (of which 3g saturates), 36g carbohydrate per serving

butter to grease
125g (4oz) milk chocolate
50g (2oz) white chocolate
150g (5oz) prune purée
200g (7oz) light muscovado sugar

3 large egg whites
1tsp vanilla extract
65g (2½oz) plain flour, sifted
icing sugar to dust

1 Preheat the oven to 180°C (160°C fan oven) mark 4. Grease a 15cm (6in) square shallow cake tin and baseline with greaseproof paper.

2 Melt the milk chocolate (see page 13). Remove from the heat and leave to cool slightly. Chop the white chocolate.

3 Mix the prune purée with the muscovado sugar. Add the egg whites, vanilla extract and melted chocolate. Fold in the flour and white chocolate.

4 Spread the mixture in the prepared tin and bake for 1 hour or until firm to the touch. Remove from the oven and leave to cool in the tin. Turn out, dust with icing sugar and cut into 12 squares.

White Chocolate and Macadamia Nut Brownies

Hands-on time: 20 minutes, plus cooling · Cooking time: 30–35 minutes

Serves 12: 510 cals; 31g fat (of which 11g saturates); 52g carbohydrate per brownie

75g (3oz) unsalted butter, plus extra
  to grease
500g (1lb 2oz) good-quality white
  chocolate, roughly chopped
3 large eggs
175g (6oz) golden caster sugar

175g (6oz) self-raising flour
pinch of salt
175g (6oz) macadamia nuts, roughly
  chopped
1tsp vanilla extract

1 Preheat the oven to 190°C (170°C fan oven) mark 5. Grease a 19 × 27cm (7½ × 10½in) baking tin and line with greaseproof paper.

2 Melt 125g (4oz) white chocolate with the butter (see page 13), stirring occasionally. Take the bowl off the pan and leave to cool slightly.

3 Whisk the eggs and sugar together in a large bowl until smooth, then gradually beat in the melted chocolate mixture; the consistency will become quite firm. Sift the flour and salt over the mixture, then fold in together with the nuts, the remaining chopped chocolate and the vanilla extract.

4 Turn the mixture into the prepared tin and level the surface. Bake for 30–35 minutes until risen and golden and the centre is just firm to the touch – the mixture will still be soft under the crust; it firms up on cooling. Remove from the oven and leave to cool in the tin. Turn out and cut into 12 squares. Store in an airtight container for up to one week.

Sticky Pear and Chocolate Brownie Cake

Hands-on time: 25 minutes · Cooking time: 1 hour

Serves 8: 470 cals, 31g fat (of which 15g saturates), 46g carbohydrate per serving

275g (10oz) plain chocolate
75g (3oz) pecan nuts
125g (4oz) unsalted butter
2 medium eggs
75g (3oz) caster sugar
½tsp vanilla extract
1tbsp strong black coffee

75g (3oz) self-raising flour, sifted
700g (1½lb) ripe pears or two 400g cans
     pear quarters, drained

For the icing
75g (3oz) golden icing sugar
2tsp strong black coffee

1 Preheat the oven to 190°C (170°C fan oven) mark 5. Grease a 1.1 litre (2 pint) 23cm (9in) round ovenproof dish and baseline with greaseproof paper. Roughly chop 75g (3oz) chocolate and the nuts. Melt the remaining chocolate and the butter (see page 13). Remove from the heat and cool slightly.

2 Beat the eggs, caster sugar, vanilla extract, 1tbsp coffee and the melted chocolate. Fold in the flour, chopped chocolate and nuts and mix well.

3 Peel, quarter and core the pears and arrange in the prepared dish. Pour over the chocolate mixture.

4 Bake for 1 hour, covering lightly with foil after 30 minutes. Cool slightly, then place a plate over the top of the dish and invert.

5 For the icing, beat the icing sugar with the coffee until smooth, adding a few drops of water if necessary to give a creamy consistency. Drizzle on to the brownie so it falls down the side. Leave to set. Serve with ice cream.

CELEBRATION CAKES

Every celebration deserves a cake and these decadent and truly special cakes will be just right for any occassion. The Wicked Chocolate Cake is a rich chocolate cake drizzled with chocolate ganache and decorated with sugared almonds – who could forget that? The Italian Ice Cream Cake contains ingredients everyone loves in one dish – chocolate, cherries, nuts, cream and boozed-soaked sponge. Add tall fine candles for extra drama!

Simnel Cake

The Easiest-Ever Celebration Chocolate Cake

Creamy Coffee and Praline Gateau

Wicked Chocolate Cake

Celebration Cake

Triple-Chocolate Meringue Cake

Pecan, Maple and Whisky Pie

Italian Ice Cream Cake

Simnel Cake

Hands-on time: 1½ hours, plus setting · Cooking time: 2¼ hours, plus cooling

Serves 12–16: 760-570 cals, 30–23g fat (of which 13–9g saturates), 118–88g carbohydrate per serving

250g (9oz) unsalted butter, softened, plus
    extra to grease
grated zest of 2 lemons
250g (9oz) golden caster sugar
4 large eggs, beaten
250g (9oz) plain flour
½tsp ground mixed spice
75g (3oz) ground almonds
50g (2oz) candied citrus peel, finely
    chopped

150g (5oz) currants
300g (11oz) sultanas
75g (3oz) natural glacé cherries, halved
100g (3½oz) icing sugar, plus extra to dust
600g (1lb 5oz) almond paste (see page 17)
    or ready-made white marzipan
2tbsp thin honey, warmed
1 egg, beaten, to glaze

1 Preheat the oven to 170°C (150°C fan oven) mark 3. Grease a 20cm (8in) round, 7.5cm (3in) deep cake tin and line with greaseproof paper.

2 Using a freestanding mixer or handheld electric whisk, beat the butter and lemon zest together until very soft. Add the caster sugar gradually and continue beating until light and fluffy. Slowly beat in the eggs until evenly incorporated.

3 Sift in the flour with the mixed spice, and add the ground almonds, candied peel, currants, sultanas and glacé cherries. Using a large metal spoon, fold the ingredients together until evenly combined. Set aside.

4 Spoon just over half the cake mixture into the prepared tin and smooth the surface. Roll out 200g (7oz) almond paste on a surface dusted with icing sugar to an 18cm (7 inch) round.

5 Put the almond paste round on top of the mixture in the tin, then cover with the remaining cake mixture. Smooth the surface and make a slight hollow in the centre, then brush lightly with cold water. Wrap a double layer of brown paper around the outside of the tin and secure with string. Bake for 1¼ hours. Cover with greaseproof paper, reduce the oven temperature to 150°C (130°C fan oven) mark 2 and bake for a further 1½ hours or until cooked to the centre.

6 Leave to cool in the tin for 1 hour, then transfer to a wire rack to finish cooling. Wrap in greaseproof paper and store in an airtight container for up to two weeks.

7 When ready to decorate, roll out 200g (7oz) almond paste to a 20cm (8in) round. Cut a 7.5cm (3in) round from the centre and add this piece to the remaining almond paste. Brush the top of the cake with honey, cover with the almond paste ring and press down. Crimp the edge with your fingers.

8 Divide the rest of the almond paste into 11 or 12 pieces and shape into oval balls. Brush the ring with the beaten egg, position the balls on top and brush them with egg. Put a disc of foil over the exposed centre of the cake, then put under a hot grill for 1–2 minutes to brown the almond paste.

9 Mix the icing sugar with 2–3tbsp warm water to make a smooth icing. Remove the foil disc, then pour the icing on to the exposed centre and smooth it with a palette knife. Leave the icing to set. To finish, secure a yellow ribbon around the side of the cake.

COOK'S TIP: Simnel cake is the classic Easter celebration cake, its marzipan balls representing the disciples – either 11 or 12 – depending on whether you think Judas should be included.

The Easiest-Ever Celebration Chocolate Cake

Hands-on time: 40 minutes, plus cooling · Cooking time: 1¼ hours

Serves 16: 170 cals, 9g fat (of which 3g saturates), 17g carbohydrate per serving

butter to grease
200g (7oz) plain chocolate, broken into
  pieces
5 large eggs
125g (4oz) golden caster sugar

100g (3½oz) ground almonds
1tbsp coffee liqueur, such as Tia Maria
cocoa powder and fresh raspberries to
  decorate
fresh raspberries to serve

1 Grease and line a 12.5 × 8cm (5 × 3⅓in) deep round cake tin with greaseproof paper, making sure the paper comes 5–7.5cm (2–3in) above the tin.

2 Melt the chocolate (see page 13). Cool. Meanwhile, preheat the oven to 170°C (150°C fan oven) mark 3.

3 Separate all but one of the eggs, putting the whites to one side. Put the yolks, the remaining whole egg and the sugar in the bowl of a freestanding mixer. Whisk at high speed for 5 minutes or until the mixture is pale and leaves a ribbon trail.

4 Set the mixer to a very low speed, add the chocolate and then the almonds and mix until evenly combined. Put to one side.

5 Whisk the egg whites until they form soft peaks. Beat one quarter of the egg whites into the chocolate mixture to loosen, then fold in the rest.

6 Pour the mixture into the prepared tin. Bake for 1 hour 5 minutes to 1¼ hours or until a skewer inserted into the centre of the cake for 30 seconds comes out hot with a few crumbs on it. Make several holes in the cake with the skewer, then pour over the liqueur while still hot. Leave to cool in the tin for 30 minutes, then turn out on to a cooling rack and leave until cold. Wrap the cake in foil and store in an airtight container for up to five days.

7 Transfer to a plate and dust with cocoa powder. Spoon raspberries on top and tie a ribbon around the cake.

Creamy Coffee and Praline Gateau

Hands-on time: 45 minutes, plus cooling · Cooking time: 25 minutes
Serves 8: 730 cals, 42g fat (of which 23g saturates), 85g carbohydrate per serving

50g (2oz) unsalted butter, melted, plus extra
    to grease
125g (4oz) plain flour, sifted, plus extra to
    dust
4 large eggs, separated
125g (4oz) golden caster sugar
1tbsp rich-flavoured coffee granules,
    dissolved in 2tsp boiling water

For the praline
150g (5oz) caster sugar
50g (2oz) whole blanched hazelnuts

For the filling
2tbsp rich coffee granules dissolved in 1tbsp
    boiling water
2 × 250g tubs mascarpone cheese
250g (9oz) golden icing sugar, sifted

1 Preheat the oven to 190°C (170°C fan oven) mark 5. Grease two 18cm (7in) loose-base sandwich tins. Dust lightly with flour and tip out excess.

2 Whisk the egg whites until they form soft peaks. Whisk in one egg yolk; repeat with the other three yolks. Add the golden caster sugar, 1tbsp at a time, and continue to whisk. Lift the whisk – the mixture should be thick enough to leave a trail. Fold half the flour into the mixture with a large metal spoon. Mix the coffee into the melted butter, then pour around the edge of the mixture. Add the remaining flour and gradually fold in. Divide the mixture between the prepared tins and bake for 25 minutes until risen and firm to the touch. Turn out on to wire racks and leave to cool.

3 For the praline top, melt the white caster sugar in a heavy-based pan over a low heat, shaking the pan once or twice to help the sugar dissolve evenly. Cook until it forms a dark golden brown caramel. Line a baking sheet with parchment and scatter over the nuts. Pour over the caramel and leave to cool.

4 For the filling, dissolve the coffee in 1tbsp boiling water. Put the mascarpone and icing sugar in a large bowl and add the coffee. Mix with an electric hand whisk. Slice each cake in half horizontally. Put one layer on to a cake platter and spread with a quarter of the filling. Continue layering to sandwich the whole cake together, finishing with a layer of the mascarpone icing on top.

5 Break the praline into two or three pieces and put into a plastic bag. With a rolling pin, smash into smaller pieces. Use to decorate the top of the cake.

Wicked Chocolate Cake

Hands-on time: 50 minutes, plus cooling · Cooking time: 1¼ hours

Serves 16: 430 cals, 28g fat (of which 15g saturates), 41g carbohydrate per serving

125g (4oz) white marzipan
225g (8oz) dark chocolate (minimum 70% cocoa solids), broken into pieces
175g (6oz) unsalted butter
175g (6oz) golden caster sugar
5 medium eggs, lightly beaten
125g (4oz) self-raising flour, sifted
3tbsp cocoa powder, sifted
4tbsp amaretto

For the ganache coating
175g (6oz) plain chocolate, broken into pieces
75g (3oz) unsalted butter
4tbsp double cream, warmed

For the decoration
12 lilac sugar-coated almonds

1 Preheat the oven to 190°C (170°C fan oven) mark 5. Freeze the marzipan for 30 minutes to firm up and make grating easier. Grease a 20.5cm (8in) spring-release cake tin and line with greaseproof paper. Melt the dark chocolate in a heatproof bowl set over a pan of gently simmering water.

2 Cream together the butter and sugar in a freestanding electric mixer until pale and fluffy. Gradually beat in three eggs – don't worry if the mixture curdles. Sift in 3tbsp flour and all the cocoa powder, then gradually beat in the remaining eggs. Fold in the rest of the flour.

3 Grate the chilled marzipan and crumble into the cake mixture. Pour all the melted chocolate into the mixture, then stir in using a large metal spoon, making sure it's evenly distributed. Add 2tbsp amaretto and stir thoroughly to combine.

4 Turn the mixture into the prepared tin, spread evenly and bake for 45 minutes. (If the cake is browning too quickly, cover it with foil.) If necessary, continue to cook for an extra 5–10 minutes or until a skewer inserted into the centre comes out clean. Cool in the tin for 30 minutes.

5 Remove the cake from the tin and cool on a wire rack, then drizzle with the remaining amaretto. To make the ganache coating, melt the chocolate (see page 13). Add the butter and warm cream and stir everything together until smooth.

6 Position the cake and rack over a tray and spoon the warm ganache coating over the top, letting it trickle down the cake sides. Use a palette knife to spread the ganache evenly over the cake. Decorate with sugar-coated almonds and store in an airtight container. Eat within one week

Celebration Cake

Hands-on time: 1½ hours, plus cooling · Cooking time: around 1 hour 25 minutes

Serves 30: 290 cals, 11g fat (of which 6g saturates), 47g carbohydrate per serving

350g (12oz) unsalted butter, softened, plus
   extra to grease
350g (12oz) golden caster sugar
6 medium eggs, beaten
350g (12oz) self-raising flour, sifted
2tbsp vanilla extract
¼ tsp salt
175g (6oz) plain flour, sifted

For the icing
4–6tbsp apricot glaze

500g (1lb 2oz) golden icing sugar
1 medium egg white
2tbsp liquid glucose, warmed (stand jar in a
   bowl of boiling water for 5 minutes)
1tsp vanilla extract

For the decoration
1 egg white, lightly beaten
3 full-blown rose heads
25g (1oz) golden granulated sugar
ribbon to decorate

1 Preheat the oven to 170°C (150°C fan oven) mark 3. Grease and line a 7.5cm (3in) deep, 23cm (9in) square cake tin with non-stick greaseproof paper. Wrap the tin in a double thickness of brown paper. Beat the butter and sugar in a bowl until light and fluffy. Add the eggs, one at a time, mixing well between each addition. If the mixture looks like curdling, add 2tbsp flour. Mix in the vanilla extract. Add 1tbsp water, the salt and the remaining flours, then fold everything together. Spoon the mixture into the prepared tin, level the surface and make a dip in the middle. Bake for 1 hour 15–25 minutes or until a skewer inserted into the centre of the cake for 30 seconds comes out clean.

2 Leave the cake in the tin for 20 minutes, then turn out on to a rack and leave to cool completely. Carefully peel off the lining paper and turn the cake over. Use a sharp knife to slice the top off the cake where it's risen, then turn the cake over again. Brush the apricot glaze over the top and leave to set.

3 Whiz the icing sugar in a food processor for 30 seconds to break up lumps. Add the egg white, glucose and vanilla extract and whiz for 2–3 minutes until the mixture forms a ball. Roll out the icing on a surface dusted with icing sugar to a 25.5cm (10in) square. Cut out a 23cm (9in) square of icing. Lift on to the cake and crimp the edges.

4 For the roses: beat the egg white in a bowl until slightly frothy. Put the roses on to a rack, brush the petals with a little egg white and sprinkle with sugar. Leave to dry for 30 minutes, then put on the cake. Finish with ribbon.

Triple-Chocolate Meringue Cake

Hands-on time: 15 minutes, plus chilling · Cooking time: 1½ hours

Serves 10: 800 cals, 58g fat (of which 32g saturates), 66g carbohydrate per serving

5 medium eggs
150g (5oz) icing sugar
40g (1½oz) cocoa powder
225g (8oz) caster sugar
175g (6oz) dark chocolate (minimum 70%
   cocoa solids)

150g (5oz) unsalted butter, softened
2tbsp liqueur, such as Drambuie
568ml carton double cream
175g (6oz) white chocolate
chocolates and truffles to decorate

1 Preheat the oven to 150°C (130°C fan oven) mark 2. Line two baking sheets with non-stick baking parchment.

2 For the meringue, separate the eggs and sift together the icing sugar and cocoa powder. Whisk the egg whites until they form stiff peaks, then slowly whisk in 150g (5oz) caster sugar. Fold in the cocoa powder and icing sugar with a large metal spoon. Spread two 23cm (9in) circles of meringue on to the baking sheets. Bake for 1½ hours until dried out. Leave to cool.

3 To make the chocolate mousse filling, melt the dark chocolate (see page 13). Stir in 75g (3oz) butter and the liqueur. Whisk three egg yolks with the remaining caster sugar until pale and thick. Lightly whip half the cream to soft peaks. Fold the chocolate into the egg yolk mixture, then fold in the cream. Cover and chill for 30 minutes, then sandwich the meringue rounds together with the mousse. Chill.

4 To complete, melt the white chocolate as above, then stir in the remaining butter and egg yolks. Lightly whip the remaining cream and fold in the chocolate mixture. Cover the meringue with the white chocolate cream and chill overnight. Decorate with chocolates or truffles.

Pecan, Maple and Whisky Pie

Hands-on time: 40 minutes, plus chilling · Cooking time: 1 hour 20 minutes
Serves 6–8: 880 cals, 58g fat (of which 22g saturates), 81g carbohydrate per serving

225g (8oz) plain flour, sifted, plus extra for
    rolling out
225g (8oz) butter
200g (7oz) pecan nuts
3 medium eggs
75g (3oz) dark muscovado sugar
1tsp cornflour

50ml (2fl oz) maple syrup
225ml (8fl oz) golden syrup
4tbsp whisky
1tsp vanilla extract
maple syrup and ice cream or whipped
    cream to serve

1 To make the pastry, put the flour and 150g (5oz) of the butter in a food processor and pulse until the mixture looks like fine crumbs. Add 3tbsp iced water, pulse until the mixture comes together in a ball, then wrap in clingfilm and chill for 30 minutes. Place the nuts on a baking sheet and lightly toast under a preheated grill. Cool, then roughly chop.

2 Roll the pastry out on a lightly floured worksurface and line a 23cm (9in) loose-base tart tin. Prick the base well, line with greaseproof paper and baking beans and chill for 30 minutes.

3 Preheat oven to 200°C (180°C fan oven) mark 6. Bake the pastry cases for 15 minutes, then remove the paper and beans and bake for another 15 minutes or until golden. Beat the eggs together and use a little to brush over the base and sides of the pastry. Return to the oven for 3–4 minutes. Set aside.

4 Beat the remaining butter with the sugar until light, then slowly add the remaining beaten eggs and the cornflour. Stir in the maple syrup, golden syrup, whisky and vanilla extract. (Don't worry if the mixture appears curdled.) Mix in the toasted pecan nuts and pour into the cooked pastry case.

5 Reduce the oven temperature to 180°C (160°C fan oven) mark 4 and bake the pie for 45 minutes or until the filling is just set. Leave to cool slightly. Serve drizzled with maple syrup, accompanied by ice cream or whipped cream.

Italian Ice Cream Cake

Hands-on time: 40 minutes, plus freezing · Cooking time: none

Serves 10: 540 cals, 37g fat (of which 16g saturates), 47g carbohydrate per serving

400g (14oz) fresh cherries, stoned and quartered
4tbsp amaretto liqueur
10tbsp crème de cacao liqueur
200g packet (containing 24) Savoiardi biscuits or sponge fingers
5 medium egg yolks
150g (5oz) golden caster sugar
450ml (15fl oz) double cream, lightly whipped

1tbsp vanilla extract
75g (3oz) pistachios or hazelnuts, roughly chopped in a food processor
75g (3oz) dark chocolate (minimum 70% cocoa solids) roughly chopped in a food processor
2–3tbsp cocoa powder
2–3tbsp golden icing sugar

1 Put the cherries and amaretto in a bowl, stir, cover with clingfilm and leave while you assemble the other ingredients. Pour the crème de cacao into a shallow dish and take out a large chopping board. Quickly dip a sponge finger into the liqueur – on one side only, so it doesn't go soggy and fall apart – then put on to the board and cut in half lengthways to separate the sugary side from the base. Repeat with each biscuit.

2 Take a 24 × 4cm (9½in × 1½in) round tin and double line it with clingfilm. Arrange the sugar-coated sponge finger halves, sugar side down, on the base of the tin. Drizzle with any remaining crème de cacao.

3 Put the egg yolks and caster sugar into a bowl and whisk with an electric mixer until pale, light and fluffy. Fold in the cream, vanilla extract, pistachios or hazelnuts, the chocolate and cherries, plus any remaining amaretto. Spoon the mixture on top of the sponge fingers in the tin.

4 Cover the ice cream filling with the remaining sponge finger halves, cut side down. Cover with clingfilm and freeze for at least 5 hours.

5 To serve, upturn the cake on to a serving plate. Ease away the clingfilm and discard. Sift the cocoa powder and icing sugar over the top of the cake and cut into wedges. Before serving, leave at room temperature for 20 minutes, if the weather is warm, 40 minutes at cool room temperature, or 1 hour in the fridge to allow the cherries to defrost and the ice cream to become 'semi-freddo' – half-frozen yet moussey (see picture on page 6).

Index

Photography Credits

All photography by William Reavell

Except for:

Michael Paul: page 6

Craig Robertson: page 13

Clive Streeter: page 1

Philip Webb: page 66

Publisher's Acknowledgements

Project Editor: Carly Madden

Design Manager: Gemma Wilson

Senior Production Controller: Morna McPherson

Layout: Ben Cracknell Studios

Home Economist and Stylist: Joanna Farrow

Nutritional Analysis: Wendy Doyle

Editorial Team: Karen Fitzpatrick, Barbara Dixon, Sandra Shotter